Never Too Early to Write

Adventures in the K-1 Writing Workshop

Bea Johnson

MAUPIN
HOUSE

Never Too Early to Write:
Adventures in the K-1 Writing Workshop

Author Bea Johnson is an elementary teacher with more than 25 years' experience in kindergarten, second grade, third grade, and first- and second-grade Chapter 1 remedial reading. Bea teaches two-day writing and social studies workshops for educators at the University of Sioux Falls. She has worked as a writing consultant for numerous schools throughout the Midwestern United States.

Editor: Candace Nelson
Cover design: Maria Messenger
Book Design: Billie J. Hermansen

Library of Congress Cataloging-in-Publication Data

Johnson, Madeline.
    Never too early to write : adventures in the K-1 writing workshop
  / Bea Johnson.
      p.   cm.
    Includes bibliographic references (p.).
    ISBN 0-929895-31-2
    1. English language--Composition and exercises--Study and teaching
(Preschool) 2. English language--Composition and exercises--Study
and teaching (Primary) I. Title.
  LB1140.5.L3J65 1999
  372.62'3044--dc21   99-15281
                                                  CIP

Maupin House Publishing, Inc.
PO Box 90148
Gainesville, FL 32607
1-800-524-0634 / 352-373-5588
352-373-5546 (fax)
www.maupinhouse.com
info@maupinhouse.com

Publishing Professional Resources that Improve Classroom Performance

10 9 8 7 6

Dedication

This book is dedicated to the memory of my parents,
Ross and Marvel Ballou,
who encouraged literacy from day one;
to my husband, Eldon,
who persuaded me to write this book in the first place;
to my kids, Judie and Lyle, and their spouses, Rick and Beth,
who told me to go for it;
to my colleagues who cheered me on;
and as always to my super students—You're the best!

Acknowledgments

*I wish to acknowledge the help of several language-arts teachers
in the Sibley-Ocheyedan School System.
Sara, Joe, and Ken steered me in the right direction,
and Sandy brought it down to my level.*

*I am also grateful for the knowledgeable advice
given me by my publisher, Julia Graddy.*

*A special thank-you to Marcia Freeman
for editing help and good practical advice.
I owe you big-time.*

*Thanks must also be given to Nancy Loyd.
Where would this book be without you
and your South Dakota connection?*

*I can't forget to thank the love of my life, Eldon,
for putting up with late meals
and the distracted glaze in my eyes.*

Table of Contents

Introduction

Why would a teacher change her teaching methods?

It has been said that change takes place when pain becomes so great that it cannot be ignored.

I reached that point of pain after I had been teaching kindergarten for eight years.

Up to that time my principal's evaluations of my teaching practices were all positive. I was following the guidelines of our school's curriculum. I was a caring teacher. I felt I knew something about the capabilities of kindergarten children.

Yet at the end of every school day, I felt a sense of loss. I was filled with guilt. Was I teaching my students correctly? Had I met their needs today? Some days I couldn't even remember if I had talked to each child.

It was at this time that I started working on my master's degree. During the course of my studies I read assigned articles by Donald Graves and Lucy Calkins. Their writings made me feel even more guilty. I suddenly had a glimmer of a great area of learning that I was passing up because I had never allowed my kindergarten students to write creatively!

I had assumed (and I was not alone in this) that the writing process could not be taught to kindergarten students before they could recognize letters, sounds, and words.

Graves and Calkins said that children could be taught to write before they learned all their letters and sounds.

Other researchers went further, stating that children who were taught to write before they learned to read became better readers later on. They attributed the reasons for this astounding statement to the fact that regular writing experiences tend to increase readiness skills, communication skills, and higher level thinking skills.

I was very interested in seeing my students do well in all these areas, but I had no idea where to start.

The more I read of the research, the angrier I felt. It was easy for Graves and Calkins to tell teachers what they should be doing from their ivy-covered towers. Sure, they went into selected classrooms and worked with a few kids, and seemingly had success. But the regular teacher was always there hovering in the background managing the rest of the class. Could a regular classroom teacher actually run a meaningful writing program and still have her class under control?

After reading piles of research on the subject of writing with young children, I decided to write my thesis on early writing. I would try to formulate an inexpensive, year-long writing program for kindergarten students using the writing researchers' suggestions. At the end of the year I would report the results of my experience and either prove or disprove the writing researchers' words.

I truly expected the program to flop. I even entertained ideas of sending my finished research to Graves and Calkins with a big "So There!" written across it.

The results of that year's experience were published in my thesis titled "Teaching the Writing Process in the Kindergarten Classroom."

To my surprise, the class responded far above my wildest expectations. Joy and intrinsic motivation were evident as they wrote. (See Figures 1, 2, 3). The end-of-year reading-readiness tests indicated that the students had a solid understanding of sound-symbol relationships, probably because the writing experience gave the letters and sounds deeper meaning.

Meaningful learning is more readily retained, as every education major can tell you.

Overall, the results of my research indicated that teaching kindergarten children to write enhanced pre-reading and readiness skills.

The idea for this book was originally conceived because a group of teachers in Worthington, Minnesota, wanted to begin writing with young children. One of my kindergarten students had moved to Worthington. The little girl's mother told the first-grade teacher how her daughter had been taught to write. The first-grade teachers told the kindergarten teachers.

Soon after, I received a call asking me to make a presentation at their school.

Eight to ten teachers came to the workshop looking somewhat skeptical. But after I had finished my hour session, and they drilled me with questions for another hour, I felt encouraged. Hearing me tell about my successes and failures seemed to reassure them. If I could do it, anybody could. They became more interested and enthusiastic as the evening progressed.

Their two principals sat in the back of the room whispering while I gave my presentation. It was unnerving. Afterwards, as they approached me, I experienced trepidation, wondering about their reaction to the writing program.

To my surprise, one of them whispered, "This is just what we needed. These teachers have been wanting to try this, but didn't know where to start or what to do. You've shown them it can be done."

This book then was born for two reasons:

- To show teachers, administrators, and parents how to have a successful year-long writing program.

- To demonstrate that a very valuable literacy tool is not expensive. It is Cheap! This program comes with a very low price tag. (The price of this book!) It utilizes reading-readiness materials already in use and requires no special teaching aids.

A special note ought to be made about the illustrations in this book. They were all created by my students. You will notice my printing interspersed with the children's scribbles, drawings, and temporary spelling. I printed what each child dictated to me when asked, "What have you written?"

Teachers may wonder what I took out of my kindergarten curriculum so that I was able to incorporate the writing program. I removed a lot of boring work sheets that were of dubious educational value. I also deleted numerous cut-and-paste activities that were not missed at all.

My beautiful students cooperated enthusiastically. And I'm grateful to their parents for accepting my writing program. Thanks are also due to the Staff of the Franklin Elementary School who cheered me on when I faltered, and to our school administrators who allowed my research.

There are several reasons I expanded the book's focus from only kindergarten to include first grade.

After self-publishing an earlier version of this book, I received mail and phone calls from first grade teachers wondering if they could use the book too. The answer was yes. Since writing is developmental, the strategies I recommend in my program can extend to higher grades. The children enter the writing experience at their own level of expertise when they are ready.

Of course you expect that most first grade children's writing will be more advanced at the end of the year. But even some third-grade children will still use pictures to centralize their thoughts, so be prepared for anything.

I can honestly say that the most important thing the writing program accomplished in my teaching was to rid me of the guilt that had troubled me. I don't go home after a busy school day wondering if I've really done my job anymore.

If you follow this program, you are forced to touch base with each child every day. The personal aspects of writing will bring you into a closer relationship with each of your pupils. You will know your students very well and will appreciate their efforts profoundly. And finally, you will be a better teacher because you have taken the time and effort to introduce your students to literacy in an enjoyable way.

Happy writing!

Figure 1: *The child expresses her delight in writing by creating a riddle about a large paper-covered box she has brought.*

Figure 2: While writing the child expresses her enjoyment of school activities.

Ready... Why Write Early?

Children who write before they read become better readers than those who don't.

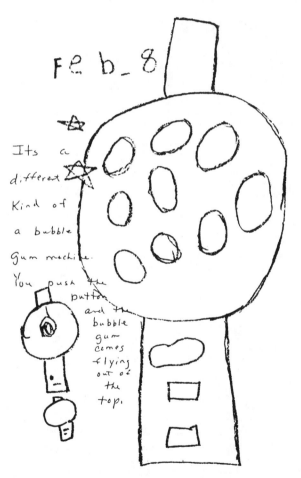

In the child's handwriting:

Feb 8

Its a
differet
Kind of
a bubble
gum machine.
You push the
button
and the
bubble
gum
comes
flying
out of
the
top.

The child considers how to invent a different type of gumball machine.

April 10, 1987
I took
tack my and serd sied
a outside and I plat it.
now It looks like This
and now it looks like
This! This

I like to write writ
Saturday
Saar day We are
going circus
goelgni to the cBrca
and I like
School! I like
house Tol

Figure 3: The child writes about and illustrates a science experiment
she conducted. She also expresses her delight in writing and
at school.

Chapter 1

Setting the Writing Stage

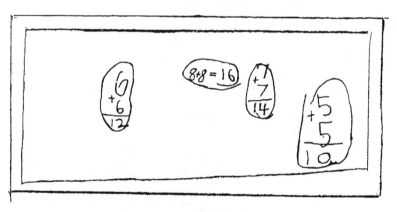

Drawing by Adam Prins
Third Grade

What's the Big Deal About Writing?

Writing is a hot educational topic. Everyone seems to agree that children should be taught to write, but many educators are still not aware of how important writing really is.

- Writing effectively communicates the author's own ideas, and in doing so, builds confidence and self-esteem, and relieves frustration (see Figure 4).

- Writing represents a special style of learning because writing makes the writer organize and clarify his thoughts using highly cognitive functions (see Figure 5).

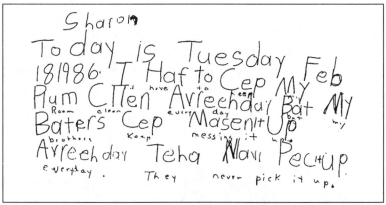

Figure 4: The child is using journal writing to express her frustrations.

Figure 5: The child writes, organizing and clarifying his thinking about Eskimo culture.

- Writing is of value in all the content areas because it makes the writer find more meaning and deeper understanding of the subject being studied. It is especially valuable in the teaching of reading.

Any good teacher of writing is also a teacher of reading because while children compose, they are reading continuously.

- You can use writing to remediate the poor reader and to analyze and diagnose reading ability.

- Writing enhances English usage, syntax, comprehension, and vocabulary.

- Writing can be used to integrate content areas so that you use the language-arts block more effectively.

Should Kindergarten and First-Grade Children Be Taught to Write?

Even when teachers are aware of the value of writing, they may be reluctant to teach it in the classroom, especially in kindergarten and first-grade classrooms. Many people assume writing should not be taught as a skill at the K-1 level because they believe children must be able to spell and read before they can write their own communications.

Others disagree. Calkins and Graves and other researchers believe that children do not need to know every sound or even how to print all letters before they become writers. They say children begin their writing experience by scribbling, drawing pictures, and inventing spelling.

These researchers claim that when children write using these methods they learn reading and pre-reading skills in a meaningful context. They also realize early in life that writing is very important.

Because I had only minimal experience with teaching writing to young children, it seemed necessary to research this subject. If the writing experience could do what the experts say it would do, my class would benefit from learning to write.

Writing specialists led me to think that early introduction of writing would enhance the development of reading skills by making these skills easier to learn. While writing, the child would use letters and punctuation, and in doing so, discover their meaning. If the meaning of letters and punctuation is known to the child, learning should come more easily and be better retained.

Also, there are many levels of writing development. The teacher needs to be aware of these levels to more intelligently teach the child at her own developmental level.

With the above knowledge in mind, I decided to develop a year-long writing program that would reach all areas of the kindergarten and first-grade curriculum. This program would not be a bunch of cute little story starters, (although I did use a few), but a writing experience that I would integrate into all the kindergarten and first-grade subjects.

I would kill two birds with one stone if I were able to accomplish this because *lack of time* seems to be the teacher's biggest excuse for not teaching writing in kindergarten and first grade. For the sake of time I would integrate writing with reading, science, social studies, health, art, and physical education. The school's curriculum goals would be met, while my students would learn to write beautifully.

But how would I begin? I needed writing strategies that took into consideration the broad range of abilities in kindergarten and first-grade children. The writing program must challenge the gifted but still affirm the strugglers. I knew sharp students would make great strides with the writing experience, but I wanted average and lower functioning children to benefit also. The whole class would be brought to a higher level of expertise because of the writing program.

Another requirement of the kindergarten and first-grade writing program was the children ought to enjoy the writing experience. Introducing writing as a joyful event rather than drudgery might influence children's later attitudes toward writing.

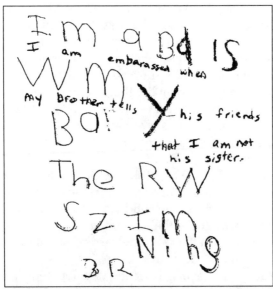

Figure 6: The child expresses feelings about her brother's behavior.

Finally, all of the above requirements would need to be useful across the curriculum express real feelings (see Figures 6, 7), be engrossing, be creative, enhance self-esteem, as well as reinforce communication, reading, thinking, and decision-making skills in order to justify inclusion in a kindergarten and first-grade writing program.

I think you'll find the following chapters fulfill all my requirements for a successful, developmentally appropriate writing program for kindergarten and first grade students.

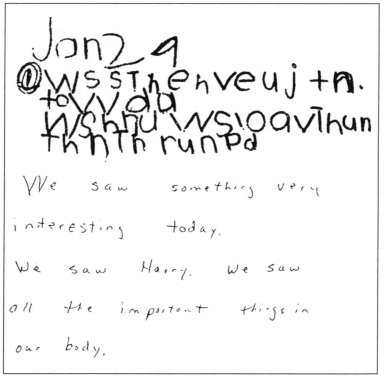

Figure 7: *The child writes about an experience with a life-sized torso model.*

Chapter 2

The Benefits of Teaching Writing in Kindergarten and First Grade

May 29, '92

Dear Kiley,
How are you? I am fine. Monday is the last day of school. School is fun! I will miss it. We have learned German this year. It was fun. Its recess now, got to go! Bye!

From,
Katie

Drawing by Katie Hartzell
Third Grade

Will a creative-writing program actually benefit kindergarten and first-grade children? Yes, in many ways!

Although there has been increased interest in the teaching of writing, many educators are still unaware of writing's impressive values. One of the reasons teachers fail to incorporate creative writing into their daily schedule is because they fail to realize the full potential of the writing experience.

In this chapter, explore the rich benefits of writing with young children.

Writing Enhances Readiness and Prereading Skills

There is much value in teaching the writing process to students even before they can print or spell. As the child takes part in language experience stories and listens to stories, (both early stages of writing), he receives exposure to print as a natural part of the learning environment.

The writing experience is especially valuable in teaching readiness skills that make print meaningful. Writing makes the child visually discriminate words while in the beginning stages of reading.

Writing enhances all the concepts a child needs to become a skilled reader. The student's vocabulary is enlarged because he uses more words in his writing than are probably found in his first reading book. Phonetics and spelling are enhanced because while children are writing words to express their personal thoughts, they are using phonics and spelling strategies.

The child who writes first will actually read earlier because writing furnishes practice using word forms and sentence patterns (see Figure 8).

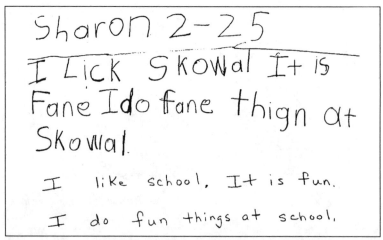

Figure 8: *A student realizes that words must be separated.*

Writers are Thinkers

Writing benefits a child's thinking process because writing actively involves the kindergarten and first-grade child in the learning process.

Writing is actually a form of thinking. If teachers who want to encourage students to be good thinkers are not using creative writing, they are missing out on the best way to get students to process information, which is especially valuable in learning. (See Figure 9.)

Figure 9: *This girl's drawing and dictation led her to a better under-standing of a question that had been bothering her.*

Writing's value to the learning process can be seen by children's scores on standardized tests. According to writing experts, students progress faster in school and score higher on these tests if they are given the opportunity to write.

What happens to the child who is not allowed to write? The latest research about the development of intelligence leads us to believe this is dangerous ground. Windows of opportunity that open only once might be missed, and potential for learning lost forever.

You can read without thinking, but you cannot write creatively without thinking. Writing forces children to think — something they sometimes seem to actively resist.

Writing Benefits Communication Skills

Communication is a key issue in this crazy world, and one of the most important concepts kindergarten and first-grade writers learn is that they can use writing to communicate with others. If children learn early in life that a communication channel is open in the form of writing, they will have advantages later. If children benefit only from the communication aspect of writing, they will be helped. Children who are allowed to write learn to communicate more effectively and rapidly. Writing becomes incredibly meaningful to students who suddenly discover they can communicate thoughts, ideas, actions, proposals, and complaints.

Communication skills are a very important outcome of the writing process because even young children have a need to share, record, and talk to themselves as well as others. Their early tries at writing reflect this need.

If early-childhood education stresses writing first, rather than reading, students will learn to communicate more quickly and effectively (see Figures 10, 11, 12, 13).

Writing Encourages Responsible Decision Making

How tough is it for a kindergarten or first-grade child to make decisions? Can they be relied on to make responsible decisions or do we need to make all their decisions for them? What effect does decision making have on a young child?

At the beginning of the kindergarten year I read aloud a children's version of a biography about Helen Keller. As the story progressed, the children saw Helen consciously making a decision to be good after realizing there was not much enjoyment in being bad.

This story leads to an introduction of the classroom rules and the importance of making right choices. (As part of my room discipline I

Figure 10: *The child uses journal writing to communicate to teacher.*

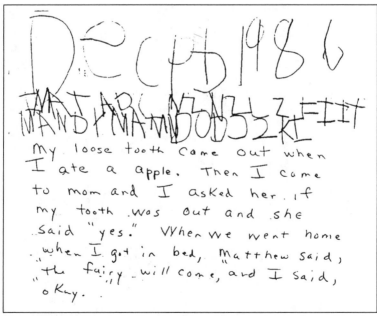

Figure 11: *Writing exactly what the child says is very important to understanding his developmental level.*

Figure 12: *The child clarifies her thinking about concepts left and right.*

Figure 13: *The child ponders what a mystery box in our classroom contains. Trying to figure out the contents of the box provoked a lot of journal entries.*

talk to children who get in trouble and try to impress them with the importance of their decisions.) Of course, some children need to be reminded of this more than others.

I use this whole decision-making idea to introduce them to writing. When the children start to write (some on the first day) they use their decision-making abilities immediately. In all my writing strategies (Chapters 6-15) children are forced to make many decisions. For example, during the *Individual Language-Experience Story* the children choose the subject and their words. *Draw and Write* demands a decision on subject, drawings, words and method of entry. *Journal Writing* allows the child to decide on subject, writing tool, form of writing (scribble, drawing, or temporary spelling), and place of writing.

Encouraging children to make responsible decisions is a major objective of our schools. Since the writing experience is all voluntary, the child is free to choose the content of his writing, or even if he will write (see Chapter 4). A non-threatening manner is essential when you introduce decision making.

Every time students write they must make several decisions. After they make their choices, they are responsible to carry through with their decisions.

What happens when teachers routinely assign topics for writing? An important benefit is stripped away from the young child. Donald Graves says that when we consistently assign writing topics, we place our students on a sort of Writing Welfare System. After a while the students don't even think about using their own ideas but become totally dependent upon the teacher. It's really difficult then for a child to feel competent enough to pick her own topics.

The long-term ramifications of responsible decision making are obvious. Giving children the freedom to make their own decisions and then to follow through on those decisions can positively affect every part of their lives.

Am I saying you should never assign topics for writing? No, there are times when you will. Don't rob children of this opportunity to acquire an important life skill (living with the results of their decisions). Your respect for children's abilities will grow as you see all the exciting and innovative choices they make without any intervention from you.

Writing Enhances Self-Esteem

Can the writing experience have any effect on the student's self-worth? Self-esteem, according to current research, is a very complex topic acquired when a child feels competent.

How does the writing experience make a child feel competent?
The child makes his own decisions.

The teacher and other students listen politely to the child's writings and respond to them in an appropriate, respectful manner.

The teacher cheers and accepts the child's writing efforts unconditionally, happy with whatever the child chooses to write.

The fact that the writing experience allows the children to enter at their own developmentally appropriate level gives children a feeling of competence because their performance will be well within their capabilities. Of course, the teacher honestly encourages and affirms each child frequently.

While the child writes, he finds out that making a mistake is not the end of the world. When a teacher models this assessment, children come to know it well. The child needs to know that even when we make mistakes, we're still worthwhile individuals. We can all learn from our mistakes and go on with life.

Children should have your attention when they need it. The conferencing aspect of the writing program gives the teacher opportunity to be one-on-one with the child each day. Since the conference encourages eye-contact, active listening, response, and affirmation of the child's efforts, it assures the child of the teacher's full attention.

Writing Helps All Areas of your Curriculum.

Teachers may complain that writing takes time. An easy answer for this problem is to use writing in every area of the curriculum.

Writing shouldn't be a once-a-week activity done on Friday afternoon, 20 minutes before the busses arrive. A truly effective writing program is done every day, and not only during writing time! Look at all the benefits mentioned already. Because writing enhances reading, thinking, decision-making, and self-esteem, it follows that the use of writing in other classes will further the understanding of whatever is being studied?

You will discover incredible truths about your teaching if you have students write in the content areas across the curriculum. It will surprise you what the children zero in on. You learn about areas where the students are totally confused. Having children write about content-area subjects can only make you a better teacher because you will know exactly what they learned and what they didn't learn.

The best thing about writing across the curriculum is that it magnifies literacy's importance to the total school experience.

Writing Vents Emotions

Most research about positive ways to vent emotions agrees that writing has a positive effect on our emotional well-being.

Do very young children have problems that need to be vented in a positive manner? They certainly do. They have joys, sorrows, grievances, frustrations, and anger, as adults do.

Can writing about something distressful actually help one emotionally and physically? The answer is yes! There are no easy answers as to why writing helps children vent emotions, but I have several ideas about the subject:

- Sometimes in the process of writing about a frustrating experience, a child senses that the whole problem was not that important.
- Writing about disagreements has a tendency to make us re-evaluate and straighten our thinking about the importance of relationships.
- Grieving students who write about situations in their lives that cannot be changed find comfort and help. The writing experience will not magically solve children's problems, but it brings them a new perspective. This perspective leads to acceptance and peace about the situation.

I received the following letter from a teacher, of which I'm going to share a part with you. I think it speaks for itself:

> The first weekend in December, the father of one of my students was killed in a hunting accident. Instead of sending flowers or memorial money, we sent Jack his very own teddy bear to "hang on to" and hug. When Jack returned to school he brought the bear with him, and the whole class got to help him pick a name for it. Jack had planned it all out as to how we would do this.

> Since we had been doing all these writing activities, his mother shared this event which I want to pass along to you. Before the funeral Jack wanted to write a letter to his dad. So with Grandmother's help he wrote the letter and had the undertaker put it in his dad's pocket so he would always have it with him. I have no idea what he wrote in that letter, but I'm sure it helped Jack deal with the sadness he felt.

> How far your writing workshop has reached around the state and into a family that has needed lots of "bear hugs" and positive ways to release their grief. Thank you so much.

Teachers should model writing about feelings to let the class know this is appropriate. Teachers should also be ready to speak directly with a child concerning a journal entry that seems distressing.

The Writing Experience Leads to Creativity

Writing provides an avenue of creativity that will be untapped if a classroom teacher is not teaching creative writing. Some students who aren't successful in any other area will be successful at writing!

The writing experience will provide an arena to showcase the outstanding abilities of some students. If writing is never done, their creativity will go undiscovered and they'll be unaware of an area of competence.

I have a saying on my classroom wall that says, "Each day, some way, each child, success."

By allowing your students to write creatively, you are giving them one more way to succeed. Plus, the original ideas they come up with will surprise, astound, and delight you.

Writing is Fun!

Children like to write because they consider it fun. If it isn't fun, the teacher is probably not following one of The Rules in Chapter 4. I tell teachers if children stop writing, at least one of these rules has been broken.

I have to admit that there are a few children who do not respond well to writing no matter what you do. When these kind of children come into my class they become a challenge. I plot all sorts of things to catch their interest.

One thing that helps is the diversity of writing strategies described in this book (Chapters 6-15). If they aren't successful with or interested in one, I'll get them with another. They will write for me. It's just a matter of time.

No child shines in all areas of writing, but most children do respond well in at least one area. I have never had a student who completely bombed in every writing genre.

During the first two years I taught writing in kindergarten I had classes who loved journaling. I remember during the second year a teacher came up to me after a workshop. His brow was knit in consternation and frustration.

"My kids aren't good at journaling," he told me in a worried tone.

I don't remember what I told him, but I know I was thinking, "Oh, you poor dear. You're obviously doing something wrong. You're probably the cause of your students' failure."

But I didn't say it out loud, thankfully. I did try to encourage him.

"Keep trying and don't give up!" I said brightly. Looking back on it, I think I probably sounded a bit smug and condescending.

The next year justice was meted out to me for my superior attitude. Yes, I had a class who really didn't enjoy journaling! I kept trying, following my own advice. Then I started to check myself out to see if I was following The Rules.

My final conclusion was that some classes like to journal better than others. Sounds simple, but it took me a long time to figure it out. It makes sense that if something isn't working, **stop it immediately**, and go on to something else.

There are two reasons for changing course at this point:

- If you persist in forcing something down children's throats, your frustrations will start to surface. This will affect your attitude about writing and it will rub off on the children.

- Some classes will do better at one strategy, like journaling. But that does not mean they will be better writers than your next class who may be more skilled in the *Draw and Write.*

Keep in mind that children *have to write* to learn to write. No one writing strategy is the pure form of writing. If your students are writing, no matter what genre they are using, you are accomplishing what you set out to do.

Writing is fun if taught with The Rules in the back of your mind. The child's initial draft of any written communication should be fun! The part that's work comes later.

Chapter 3

The Stages of Writing Development

Drawing by Dustin VandeBrake
Third Grade

Kindergarten and first-grade teachers need to know the stages of writing development. This knowledge helps the teacher recognize if a child is working up to her capabilities.

Different writing researchers describe stages of writing development according to varying criteria. For the purposes of quick, general understanding, I suggest the following benchmarks:

Stage 1: The child scribbles (see Figure 14).

Stage 2: The child writes with curvy lines, cursive m's, and a series of small circles and vertical lines. The size of an object at this stage might be shown by the size of the marks made (see Figures 15, 18).

Stage 3: The child starts to arrange letters that are known in different ways to indicate different words. There is small or no knowledge of the alphabet at this stage (see Figure 19).

Stage 4: The child starts tracing and copying and using mock-letters and symbols. He also divides words at any point, suddenly changes the direction of writing, and reverses known letters (see Figures 16, 22).

Stage 5: The child uses random lettering, labeling, and listing of key words. Temporary spelling appears. The child invents letters (mostly consonants) when he isn't sure of the correct spelling. Syllabic hypothesis starts to happen. (The child writes one letter for each syllable that he hears.) (See Figures 17, 19)

Stage 6: The child uses more alphabet letters (vowels start to appear) to form words. The temporary spelling becomes closer to standard spelling (see Figures 20, 21).

Stage 7: The child uses conventional spelling, for the most part.

Knowledge the teacher gains from information on writing stages will help individualize each child's writing program. This is an important consideration because teachers today face classes with a broader range of abilities.

The teacher needs to be aware of these indicators of writing development's natural sequence because this is not a *Pushing Program*. All the experts' research leads to the conclusion that the writing program benefits children who are functioning at a writing stage within their capabilities. Teaching children at a level they are incapable of achieving is frustrating to both the teacher and child. And research reveals dangers in teaching children as if they are all on the same level. But an effective teacher can offer just a slight nudge now and then to expand students' horizons. (There are many ways to nudge children. See Chapter 17 for my suggestions.)

A final note concerning writing levels: It is not uncommon to see children regress to a lower writing level. I observed this on many occasions in my classroom. It seems to be a normal and acceptable part of a writing program that gives students great freedom on subject

Figure 14: *Child is using journal writing to express fears. He used drawings and squiggles to compose his story and then dictated the words to the teacher.*

Figure 15: *Notice the child's dictated words: "I'm practicing cursive."*

Figure 16: *The child is experimenting with invented symbols and spelling.*

Figure 17: *The child is at the five-year, key-word stage. The child uses writing to list key words in her life.*

Figure 18: *The child delights in her drawing and her dictated story.*

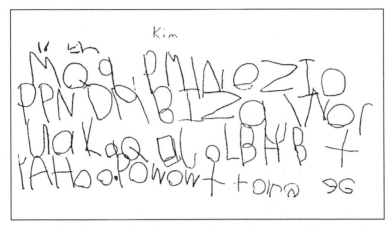

Figure 19: *Child is at the five-year stage of random lettering. She writes for the joy of just putting something down on paper.*

Figure 20: *An example of transitional spelling, where a mixture of conventional and temporary spelling are used.*

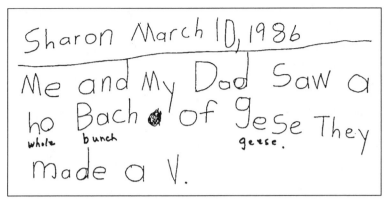

Figure 21: *Another example of temporary spelling.*

Sharon March 10, 1986

Me and My Dad Saw a ho Bach of geSe They made a V.

(whole bunch geese)

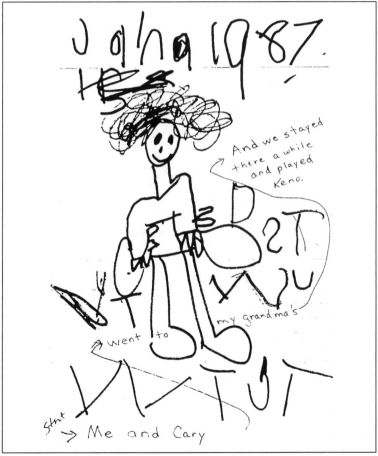

Figure 22: *As the child dictated the story to the teacher, he started at the bottom and went up.*

matter, materials, and method of writing. If the regressions seem to be abnormal, or the result of laziness, the teacher should reassess the situation and take appropriate action. Now might be the time for one of the nudges mentioned above.

In chapters 6-15 I will describe several strategies for teaching kindergarten and first-grade students to write. I incorporate these strategies into a year-long program that is both practical and workable in the ordinary classroom. My program reinforces readiness skills, gives success to every student, and addresses every area of the developmentally appropriate kindergarten and first grade curriculum.

Chapter 4

The Rules

Drawing by Lindsay Janssen
Third Grade

To effectively implement a writing program in the kindergarten and first-grade classroom, the teacher needs to know The Rules. The Rules are the principles and guidelines that make the writing experience fun and productive. These rules are based on research and my personal experience.

All students come to you wanting to write. It is teachers' responsibility to develop students' writing skills to the best of their abilities. Following the rules below guarantee a classroom writing workshop that's fun and successful.

A note of caution: These rules aren't the Ten Commandments. They aren't absolute. Because of the diversity in student personalities and learning styles, you need liberty to break these rules on occasion.

The Rules are an ideal. Probably no one will be able to follow them at all times. All the same, it is good to have them in the back of your mind as you introduce writing to young children.

Rule #1

An effective writing classroom has an informal atmosphere, supportive and accepting, where children feel free to experiment and to risk error (see Figures 23, 24). The child will have a choice of what to write about and even to decide if he will write!

"What?" I can hear teachers say. "You mean children don't have to write if they don't want to?"

Figure 23: *This child is experimenting with the period.*

Figure 24: *This child feels free to experiment with the exclamation point.*

That's correct. Oh, I'm going to try to motivate them to write with all my professional skills, but if they still choose not to write, that's okay.

In kindergarten and first grade if they come to me and say, "I can't think of anything to write," I usually say, "Just go back to your desk and think a while." By the time they get back to their desks and notice that all the kids around them are busily writing, they suddenly think of something.

One time a child came up to me during journal writing and said, "I don't feel like writing." I gave him my usual suggestion and sent him back to his desk. A few minutes later he was back at my desk saying, "Teacher, I don't feel like....," and he threw up all over me. He honestly did not feel like writing!

Give children the freedom to choose if they want to write and where (within reason) they want to write. There should also be a choice of writing instruments, and subjects. Only direct them to write about what is important to them.

Encourage students to write by accepting all writing efforts with the thought that all the scribbles, drawings, and invented spellings are another step toward the mastery of our complex English language.

Well-intentioned teachers alter the child's ongoing process of communication by telling him what to write, where to write, when to write, and with what to write. This is called "stealing ownership." Stealing ownership stops the creative process in its tracks. It damages the child's fragile self-esteem because the privilege of making decisions regarding the writing has been taken away. Children need to *hear* their own voices in print, and *see* their own voices in print.

Teachers who demand perfection and who will not allow their students freedom to experiment and to risk error will suddenly find that their students quit writing. If their students do write at all, they usually produce dull, safe writing.

Rule #2

An effective writing program has a teacher who stresses content, not spelling, neatness, and punctuation.

A teacher who pays attention only to the child's spelling, punctuation and neatness gives the impression that what the child has *said, thinks, or is,* is unimportant.

Children need experience with writing before they learn the many rules of language. Teachers need to encourage their students to focus on meaning so they'll be able to write with more freedom and joy.

Stressing neatness instead of content is an ever-present danger. Many of us were carefully taught the opposite during our school days. But especially in early childhood, all attempts at writing should be celebrated rather than corrected! Celebrating writing means zeroing in on the content. (See Chapter 8 — The Writing Conference, for a thorough discussion of Stressing Content).

A good beginning goal for kindergarten and first-grade writing is *fluency*. This means we want the kids to write lots of words. When children can sit down and put their thoughts on paper quickly and easily, they are fluent writers *even if they make errors*. If the teacher is always correcting the students' spelling and punctuation errors, the children will stop guessing and trying. This will lead to dull writing with students afraid to use words that they can't spell.

I do not wish to give the impression that I am completely unconcerned about proper letter formation. *But the fact is that being overzealous about these things can have a discouraging effect on young writers.* When the students turn in their writing I comment only on their content!

Proper letter formation is taught, but at a different time. Children are taught how to form their letters correctly during penmanship time, not creative writing time.

Guidance counselors tell teachers to help students overcome behavioral difficulties by dwelling on only one problem area at a time. Learning several new behaviors at one time is overwhelming and makes it easier for a child to give up. The same principle applies to writing. Many of us have had experiences with teachers who red-marked every error in our writing with the best of intentions. They made us feel like failures in writing. Being a bear-cat on writing skills while neglecting content is counter-productive. It will actually stop your students from writing.

Rule #3

An effective writing program encourages table talk.

This social interaction serves two important functions. *First, it reinforces the relationship between the written and the spoken language.* Teachers should not expect total silence while the children are free-writing. Children visiting while they are writing are learning that their words can be written down and that different words can be used to tell about experiences. They learn that certain topics are very interesting to other students.

Interacting with teachers and peers during writing helps the children reflect on what they have written and then revise as needed.

Positive feedback and meaningful interaction are necessary, not only between the children, but between the teacher and children as well.

As the children write, occasionally the teacher should circulate among them, listening to their conversations, observing their writing, and asking pertinent questions if the content isn't clear. The questions of the teacher and of other students during writing time cause greater reasoning and understanding in the writer's mind.

For young children, talk provides a natural entry into writing and can be used to accompany, reinforce, and supplement actions. *A classroom environment that encourages oral language as a meaningful context for learning to write enables children to observe how written language functions in a natural everyday setting.* When children serve as resources for one another, they learn about the writing process as they help each other generate ideas, spell words, invent spelling, and revise their writings.

Second, social interaction teaches the writer an awareness of audience.

To be successful writers children must be taught to apply what they have learned in a meaningful, clear way. They can do this only when they become aware that they have an audience.

As the child emerges from egocentricity, he becomes aware of audience, and he wants the audience to like what he has written. Through social interactions with their peers, children learn that what they write can be received and valued by persons other than themselves. Because of this, they develop an awareness of their audience's interests, understanding, and expectations. The young writer also learns that topics can be approached in different ways and that people can have different points of view. An example of these differing viewpoints might be when one child writes, "I like it when it rains." He is quite surprised when another child at his table remarks that she doesn't like the rain.

I cannot stress the value of social interaction enough. Teaching the relationship of the printed word to the spoken word is a prime goal of most readiness and pre-reading programs and should be fostered whenever possible.

Advise your principal and next-door teachers as to why all the talking and interaction is taking place. Be prepared for the noise level of table talk, but don't tolerate unacceptable, out-of-control behavior during writing time.

Children can learn to speak in subdued tones. I call these tones our "one-inch voices." I teach my kids to talk in one-inch voices at the beginning of each year. I model how I usually use my classroom voice when I'm talking to my students. Then I suddenly talk in subdued tones to a child right next to me. The class picks up on that swiftly. We talk about occasions when we need to use our one-inch voices. It doesn't take long for even young children to get the idea. The album *One Elephant, Deux Éléphants* by Sharon, Lois & Bram contains the song *Candy Man and Salty Dog*. This particular song instructs kids how they can even sing in a one-inch voice. Teach your class to use this soft voice by reading them the Wright Group Big Book called *The Farm Concert*. This book tells about a farmer with loud, noisy animals who tells the animals to make softer noises so he can sleep. The animals' words are written in smaller letters in the last part of the book, encouraging the children to read in a soft voice, which they do quite naturally.

Some children will prefer quiet so they can think. Be prepared to meet their needs by providing them with a quiet spot in the room, or some kind of ear gear that deadens sound. (I use unplugged earphones I check out from our school library.)

I don't wish to give the impression that I allow *all* table talk. Some table talk can distract and mislead children and harm the writing experience. If a child is disturbing others regularly, he should be moved. Use your good judgment in these cases.

Rule #4

An effective writing program has a teacher who values writing and shows it.

How do teachers show that they value anything? Can you walk into a classroom and tell quickly what a teacher values?

I think so.

It would take you two seconds to tell that I value writing by glancing around my room. The first things that meet your eye when you enter is a reading center filled with student-made books. There is a writing center labeled "The Write Spot" with all kinds of writing apparatus on display. There are sentences posted in all the areas of the room. Not just words, but sentences: "This is Mrs. Johnson's desk," etc.

What are some other ways in which teachers show they value writing? They spend time doing it. Post writing in prominent places. Publish students' writing in school publications. Submit their writing for publication in national magazines. (A list of these magazines, their addresses, the type of writing they prefer, and the age requirements for student participants, is located at the end of this book.) The experience of submitting student writings to these publications is well worth the effort. If the child's writing is published, the child will be affirmed in an unforgettable way. If the child's writing is turned down he will still feel good about your confidence in his abilities. We all have to deal with rejections throughout life. The teacher can help the child accept the situation and determine to try again.

Show students that you value their writing by reading it to the class. Make it a practice to comment on the good qualities of each shared writing and the hard work that was involved. The class should be encouraged to make positive remarks also.

Probably the most practical way of showing that writing is of value is by letting students see you use print in a relevant manner. All of the students' names should be posted somewhere in the room on the duty list, the birthday list, or on the check-in board. Objects in the room ought to be tagged and labeled in complete sentences that the children have dictated. Rules should be posted and reread occasionally. Directions should be printed daily on the board. Personal notes should be written on pupils' papers.

Students ought to be able to observe their teacher writing notes to the school secretary and parents. Sit down and write in your journal while the kids are writing. Writing in the children's presence models writing behavior. Students learn a lot about writing by example. For this same reason the principal, PE teacher, music teacher, etc. ought to come into the room when the kids are writing and sit down and write, too. If teachers and others are involved in writing and it seems meaningful, the students will know that writing is highly valued.

Share your own writings with kids occasionally. Reading original writings to the class is modeling a behavior that you want them to display. You will find this to be a fun experience because the kids love to hear your stories. I usually write about episodes from my childhood when I was a less-than-perfect child. This is highly interesting to my students for some unknown reason.

Read and post notes received from the superintendent, principal, parents, younger brothers and sisters, students who have moved away, visiting teachers, and authors.

Value writing by having your students write daily sometimes more than once.

Value writing by having one of your former student-authors from a previous year come back and read his story to the class, or have an autograph session with your class. My kids always enjoyed "big" kids coming into our room to share.

Designate an author-of-the-day. Give the author a badge and prepare a chair that is used for the author alone. Give the author-of-the-day special privileges.

For sharing time urge children to read their journal entries. This is much better than the old "show and tell" or the more common name "bring and brag."

Publish their stories, and have an author party. If the kids decide to donate their books to the school library, invite the parents to come with their cameras for this momentous occasion.

Construct all kinds of books with the children. Read about authors. See movies about authors. Find out what makes them tick. The more you can get your class to think like authors, the better writers they will become.

Urge kids to design posters and cards with a real purpose. Show them the work that other children and classes have accomplished. Challenge them to think of their own ideas, and then go ahead and do it.

Valuing writing means to literally surround them with print! The best way to influence your students to learn to write is by inundating them with the printed word.

Rule #5

An effective writing program has a teacher who provides students with the tools, time, and structure to write.

Tools

Children need to have the freedom to choose the paper they want to write on, and the writing instrument they want to use. Ideally, the child who has a choice in these areas will feel more like writing, which is what we want!

Paper

It will not surprise many teachers to know that children do not like to creatively write on traditional, wide-lined paper.

I prefer typing paper for the early writing efforts. Because this white paper doesn't inhibit imagination or create boundaries, the children feel freer to compose. I tried this and found that when children used typing paper or narrow-lined paper, they would get started writing more quickly than when they used the traditional, wide-lined, kindergarten writing paper.

One researcher stated that children write more, and with greater syntactic maturity on narrow-lined paper (such as notebook paper or theme paper) than on wide-lined penmanship paper used in many American schools. This researcher speculated that one factor affecting the flow of thought and the willingness to write long passages may be the time pupils were spending forming large letters.

Markers and Pencils

A surprise for me was how much my students loved to write with colored markers. Why do children choose markers instead of pencils? One expert speculated that the thick primary pencils used for writing in the lower grades are surprisingly difficult to use! Try to write with one and you'll see what we put the kids through. A lot of pressure is needed to make legible marks, and the marks that are made certainly are not colorful.

The latest research on the use of color in the classroom suggests that more learning occurs when we make our classroom posters, signs, displays, etc. in bright colors. It makes sense that colored markers would be more motivational than the usual, boring black lines of lead pencils.

Probably the main reason schools use large pencils is to save money. Skinny pencils are actually easier for the children to control and grasp. Most of them have been writing with them at home anyhow.

The best tool I recommend for beginning writers is the thin marking pens. Purchase 10 packages of Crayola Thin Line Markers for a class of 24. These should last the whole year.

These markers do bleed through the paper, so I had my students write on only one side of a page. If there is a problem with marks on the next page, train children to put a piece of scratch paper between the pages before they begin.

Time

Writing takes time.

The teacher's goal should never be to push children but rather to help children pursue their interests in learning and to promote a positive attitude toward writing.

Any writing involves thinking, writing, rethinking, rewriting, rereading, etc. Patience helps this process unfold. Writing is a process that cannot be hurried or forced, but must be nurtured, encouraged, and appreciated.

The nature of our school schedules makes this a tough rule to follow. I think the best way to accomplish this rule is to make accommodations that give the children free time outside of the usual writing time so they can finish what they've begun.

Also, if a child is on a roll, let him go, no matter what your schedule is. One of my students walked into school one day and said, "Teacher, I want to write a book." I quickly stapled together some pages and he went at it. He didn't stop for the pledge. He didn't stop for sharing. He wrote all the way through to the first recess.

I decided that what he was doing was much more important than anything I had planned. I couldn't justify yanking him out of that creative mode and forcing him to do the regular classroom activities. If other kids asked what he was doing, I told them. I said, "If you are ever writing a book, you can do the same thing." They looked impressed and there were no complaints. They could see that I was valuing writing by giving him the time to finish what he had started.

It didn't happen many times. Not many students are able to focus as well as this boy did. But if they have something that great going, *don't stop them.* Give them the time they need.

Structure

An effective teacher knows the structures young children use to appropriately accomplish writing.

They are the following:

- Dictation
- Scribbling
- Drawings
- Inventive Spelling

These structures will be explained thoroughly in Chapter 5.

Rule #6

An effective writing program has a teacher who is sensitive to the personal and emotional aspects of writing.

The teachers' lounge is no place to discuss the latest revelation that has appeared in your students' writing. Children need privacy and respect in regard to their writing.

Children's writings are very open and honest. Sometimes the subjects they deal with can be painful to everyone concerned.

Treat their writing like you would an adult's. If you do share them with someone else, ask the child's permission first.

Rule #7

An effective writing program should include writing activities every day.

Expertise in writing will not happen if writing is taught on Friday afternoon at 2:30. Students need daily exposure to writing experiences to develop the confidence and skills they need to handle future writing tasks.

$$\boxed{\textbf{Rule \#8}}$$

An effective early-writing program recognizes that early writings should not be graded.

If evaluations need to be made, comment only on the child's progress *compared to himself*. For instance: "Johnny entered kinder-garten using scribbles and drawings in his writing. During the first nine weeks he started using the first stage of temporary spelling. His writing is usually about real-life happenings."

The Teacher and the Eight Rules

An teacher can enhance the writing program by valuing the content of children's writings and by displaying informality, acceptance, encour-agement, sensitivity, and knowledge of the structures children use to write. This teacher will have her children write every day.

On the other hand, a teacher can have a deleterious effect on stu-dents' writing by having a once-a-week (if we have time!) writing program. This teacher obsesses about neatness, spelling, punctuation, and absolute quiet, and has unbending rules about writing tools, time, and structure.

Chapter 5

The Big Four:
Dictation, Drawing, Scribbling,
and Temporary Spelling

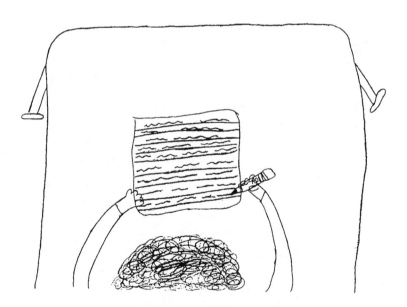

Drawing by Jackie Olthoff
Third Grade

I'm sure you have all had the experience where a child races up to you with a paper covered with scribbles clutched tightly in his fist.

"Look at my writing!" he demands.

If you were like me before my research, you would probably pat him on the head and say insincerely, "That's nice Johnny," and promptly ignore him.

Little did I know that the scribbles that Johnny wanted to share with me were a beginning stage of writing that educators and parents have long disparaged or overlooked.

What would have happened if I had asked him, "What have you written?" I would have learned what he was thinking. If I had written out his words before his eyes, he would have learned important readiness skills by observing my example.

Kindergarten and first-grade teachers have thousands of "Johnnys" running to them every year. For the most part, they fail to take advantage of the learning potential offered to them on a silver platter.

Many times children don't realize they can write. An effective writing teacher leads kids to an understanding of the four structures needed for early-childhood writing.

Are dictation, scribbling, drawing, and temporary spelling necessary to early writing development? Yes.

These four structures that children use for their early writing experiences have been greatly underrated by educators. The average teacher hears very little about them, but let's get the facts right: *It is possible to enhance children's literacy by allowing them to dictate words, sentences, and phrases; to scribble; to draw; and to come up with their own temporary spellings.*

In this chapter I will address the practical usefulness of the BIG FOUR, and observe a few examples of the last three. I will devote a greater part of my comments to the subject of temporary spelling because it is the prime objective of the kindergarten and first-grade writing program during which scribbling, drawing, and dictation are commonly employed.

Dictation

What does a child gain by watching his teacher transcribe his dictated story?

The benefits are unending. The child realizes immediately that his spoken words have meaning and can be written down. The teacher models good penmanship. The child observes left-to-right progression, punctuation, capitalization, phonics, sentence structure, word forms, etc. Self-esteem is enhanced because the child realizes that someone else is reading his words and responding to his message (see figures 27, 28).

Figure 25: *The child is using a journal entry to express grief.*

It is JOSh
Wed. FEb 19 19 86

Once at my grandpa + grandmas house, my other grandpa died. We went to the funeral and went out to bury him. I felt sad.

The child is using journal to express emotions.

Figure 26: *The child is using a journal to express emotions.*

Figure 27: The child dictates a fantasy.

Figure 28: The child relates a scary incident.

Figure 29: *The child uses a scribble, then dictates his thought.*

Drawing

Drawing is an early stage of writing. Children discover they can not only draw things but also write speech.

This leads them to the generalization that ideas in oral language can be encoded in written language.

Drawing is important because it is a manageable means the child uses to clarify thoughts and represent ideas. The student uses the drawings to choose a subject to write about because the drawing functions as a pre-writing organizer in kindergarten and first grade. Sometimes even older students will need to use drawing to clarify thoughts and form the basis and supportive structure of their writing.

Drawing becomes the child's rehearsal stage of writing. Adults are able to think abstractly about an idea and then write it. Young children are unable to do this, but they are able to draw a picture that represents their thinking.

The spontaneous drawings done by children help them express their feelings non-verbally. These drawings often show that children's internal knowledge goes beyond their intellectual knowledge.

Drawings can indicate so many things about the child's thoughts. You should observe them carefully. When they draw, children demonstrate the perceptions they are receiving and which in many cases they don't understand.

Doctors and psychologists have long been aware of the importance of drawings. The drawing process helps patients work through fears and struggles while coping with diseases.

An example from my file was drawn by a third-grade girl working though grief after her mother had miscarried a much-wanted child. (See Figure 25.) Notice the details of the hospital room with the mother crying, the father crying, the people on the TV crying. Even the sun shining through the window has a down-turned mouth.

I couldn't figure out what one little boy was trying to communicate when he came to me for his writing conference, but when he dictated the noted words (see Figure 26) I learned about a sad occasion in his life that he was still thinking about.

Drawings usually decrease during the last part of first grade, when the child reaches the stage of mental development that enables him to visualize ideas without pictures.

Scribbles

My principal walked into my room one day just as the children were beginning to write in their journals. They were happily creating their entries using scribbles, drawings, and temporary spelling. He walked around and observed a few minutes then whispered to me, "Even when they're scribbling, they're still learning something! How to hold a pencil, and how to use it!"

He was right. The oft-maligned scribbling stage of writing that appears on wallpaper, painted walls, sidewalks, and in library books, does have value in the writing process.

The child uses scribbles to experiment with the formation of letters, words, and symbols. The freedom to do this is very important as is noted in the chapter on *The Rules*.

Motor control is developed while scribbling, as my principal noticed. Some of their scribbles become so elaborate that they at times attain the level of art. Control of the writing instrument is always important to young writers' growth, so the more they use the writing instrument, the better.

The child's grip improves and the symbols used gradually change as the kindergarten year progresses. The children use scribbles to communicate information they feel is important. When my students finish writing in their journals and come to me for the student-teacher

Figure 30: *The child uses cursive-like scribbles, then dictates his message.*

conference and I ask, "What have you written?" they can immediately tell me what they were thinking about when they produced the scribble (see Figure 29).

As children scribble they are mimicking grownup writing. Usually children will scribble from left to right so directionality is also reinforced. Often children will try to indicate through scribbles the spaces between words and the configuration of sentences. (see Figure 30).

And to top it off, scribbling is fun! Even adults have been known to indulge in it. It seems to fulfill a definite need. But we don't call it "scribbling"; we call it "doodling."

Temporary Spelling

What is temporary spelling? It is children's first attempts to write words using their best judgment about spelling.

There are three stages of temporary spelling. You will become aware of them all immediately when your children start writing. The following are brief descriptions of each stage:

Stage One: The child represents words by using only the beginning sound of each word. (See Figure 31).

Figure 31: *The child is at the first stage of temporary spelling. He uses only the first consonant sound of each word to write his message.*

Stage Two: The child uses the beginning and final consonant sounds of words. (See Figure 32).

Figure 32: *This child is at the second stage of temporary spelling, using first and last and some medial sounds as he writes.*

Stage Three: The child uses the beginning and final sounds and starts filling in the vowel sounds. (See Figure 33).

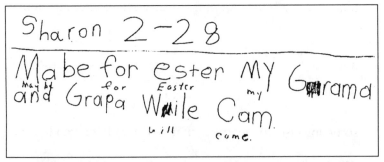

Figure 33: *This child is at Stage Three of temporary spelling. She uses first and last consonant sounds and the vowel sounds.*

Knowledge of these spelling stages is helpful because it enables you to identify the time when a child is ready for formal spelling instruction. Most spelling experts believe that children are not ready for this until they have progressed to Stage Three of temporary spelling. (More about that later in this chapter.)

What advantages does the student gain from the use of temporary spelling? Research reveals the following benefits:

- Temporary spelling moves the child naturally from readiness to regular writing using familiar symbols, the same symbols that conventional texts use. The information a child uses to execute temporary spelling transfers readily to conventional spelling and traditional reading (see Figures 34, 35, 36, 37).

- Temporary spelling removes obstacles from the path of writing and frees the child to proceed with no interruptions. This feeling of power leads to greater fluency, a prime consideration in the beginning writing experience. Temporary spelling frees the beginning writer and encourages the student to *write more and for a wider variety of purposes*.

- Temporary spelling gives the student control of and responsibility for print. These positively influence self-esteem and decision-making skills because the student feels competent.

  A second-grade-teacher friend of mine, Doris Estes, started her children journal writing at the beginning of a particular school year. She recounted to me later all the moans and groans that had accompanied the writing time during the first few weeks. But after that period, the children started to ask for the writing time and would remind her if she forgot. She felt that by following *The Rules* and allowing temporary spelling, she had provided all her students with an interesting, exciting experience that paid off at the end of the year with excellent growth in all areas of language arts.

- Temporary spelling gives efficient instruction by the child himself. The student decides what letter makes the sound in a word. If a child is unable to come up with a letter, asking someone at his table is always a good and acceptable idea. This gives each student a multitude of teachers. If the child is asked to help someone else, the learning that has already taken place is reinforced beautifully.

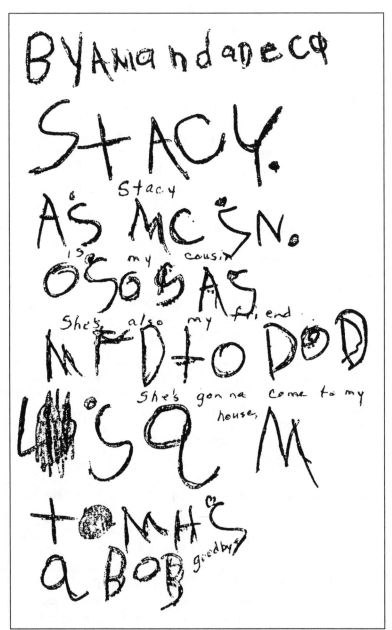

Figure 34: The child uses temporary spelling in a journal entry.

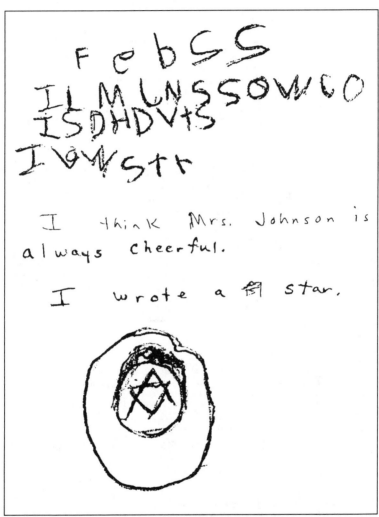

Figure 35: An example of temporary spelling during journal writing.

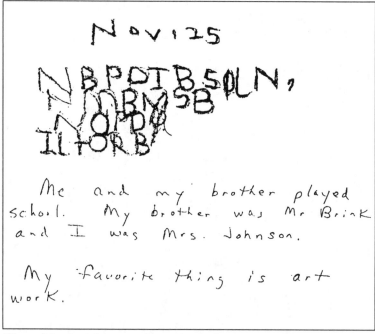

Figure 36: A child uses temporary spelling in a journal entry, then reads her words to the teacher, who quickly prints the message.

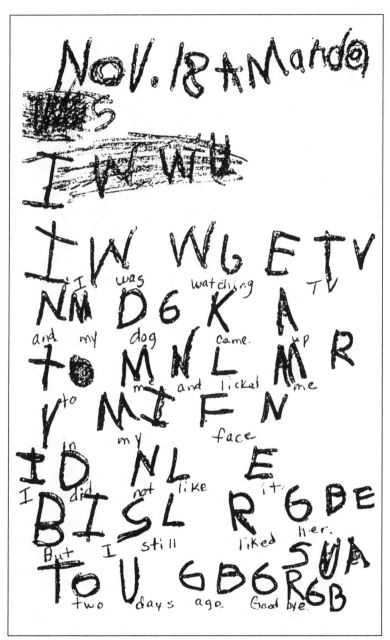

Figure 37: The teacher scribed these words directly under the
child's temporary spelling, as she read the journal entry
aloud.

- Temporary spelling improves without formal instruction for a long time. Then as the child starts observing words in his word-rich environment, spelling competence will increase.

- Temporary spelling improves sight vocabulary, word building skills, and phonics skills because it improves the child's understanding. Many teachers have noticed that phonics instruction in isolation without any purpose is ineffective. Research says that temporary spelling helps the child learn the sounds more effectively than most phonics instruction, which comes at an inappropriate time.

    Allowing the child to come up with temporary spelling and to produce written language by himself increases his under-standing. Piaget wrote that in order for children to understand something, they must construct it themselves—they must reinvent it. *Temporary spelling effectively accomplishes that goal!*

    These statements lead us to believe we have been spinning our wheels teaching phonics (as if it were the panacea for all problems) if we haven't been allowing our students to experiment with those sounds using temporary spelling. Temporary spelling gives meaning to phonics instruction and enhances understanding of the letters, sounds, and concepts being taught.

- Temporary spelling is appropriate because it is accomplished at the child's own developmental level. *This program does not push children.* Pushing kids beyond their capabilities can squash the budding writer.

- Temporary spelling better evaluates a student's auditory and visual perceptions. You know children's abilities more readily because you will see evidence of student understanding as they write each day using temporary spelling.

Questions and Answers about Temporary Spelling

Question: When can children start to use temporary spelling?
Answer: Do not make children wait to use temporary spelling until they have learned all their letters and sounds!

Experts say that children who know six sound-symbol relationships (usually consonants) can begin to write. Most children will use the letters they know and experiment cheerfully with the rest.

Question: How do you encourage children to start using temporary spelling?

Answer: Here's an easy way to introduce temporary spelling to your students: Write a message on the board in cursive and ask the children to read it. (Even the brightest kindergarten child won't be able to read cursive. Third graders even have trouble reading cursive.) When they say they can't read it, read the message to them and explain that even though they can't read it, it is nevertheless real writing.

Tell them that just as they couldn't read your writing, sometimes you will not be able to read their writing. When this happens, they may have to read it to you. To make sure you remember what they have written, you will probably have to write their words on the bottom of their writing or on a post-a-note.

Your printing of their message is *not* a correction. It is not done in red pencil. Any color of pen or pencil except red is fine. Writing children's words is simply a way that you can remember their messages. It will surprise you to know that sometimes they forget their own messages. It is important that it is written right away or their thinking at that particular moment is lost forever (see Figures 34, 35, 36, 37).

When children write with temporary spelling and you respond to their messages, you encourage them to think of themselves as writers and authors from the first day.

Model it yourself. When you're writing the Individual Language-Experience Story (ILES) (see Chapter 6) message of the day and you come to a word that you can't spell, tell the class honestly, "I don't know if this is the correct spelling, but I'm going to take a shot at it so I won't have to stop writing." Circle the problem word to remind yourself to check later with the dictionary and see if it is spelled correctly.

Model temporary spelling for groups and individuals. Let them know it is okay to guess. Remind them to listen carefully and write what they hear. Accept all their suggestions at first.

I do the temporary spelling on the board as we begin journal writing. Someone volunteers a sentence and I work through it word-by-word, calling on volunteers for the proper letter. It goes against the grain for most teachers to leave that message on the board all day, but that message will demonstrate to children that you have given them the freedom to spell words their way.

I have individual children start temporary spelling by asking them to write a familiar nursery rhyme. More advanced children could write a familiar fairy tale. Usually they're floored by the fact they can write out the rhyme or story without worrying about the proper spelling. If they ask, "Is this right?" I convince them it's fine for now, and then I tell them how extremely clever they were to come up with the spelling used.

By using the term "temporary spelling" you are letting kids know that there is a real spelling. But just as there's a grown-up way to draw something, children use their own versions to get their ideas across. Temporary spelling is a child's version of adult spelling.

Chapter 16, *Communicating the Writing Program to Parents*, provides ways to explain temporary spelling to parents. Don't just educate your students' parents, enlist them. Get them in your corner. Help them become aware of the advantages of temporary spelling. Parents also need to be aware of the fact that older brothers and sisters are sometimes the culprits in discouraging budding writers because they tease or nastily inform the little brother or sister, "You didn't spell that right!" These remarks should be seriously dealt with because they inhibit blossoming writers, and they take much of the joy out of beginning writing efforts.

Temporary spelling can be encouraged by instituting a preschool and kindergarten writing program that is developmentally appropriate. These programs will increase the number of children who engage in temporary spelling.

In the introduction to this book I wrote about first-grade teachers who inherit students who already have a year of the writing experience. Those first-grade teachers have a much easier job in teaching and introducing the program to parents.

Something interesting happened when my first kindergarten class who had experienced the writing program reached second grade. Second-grade teachers commented that many of the kids asked to write! The advantages of the writing program do carry-over into the higher grades. The earlier children are exposed to a writing program, the more carry-over will occur.

Temporary spelling can be enhanced by letting the children see and hear pieces from other students who are at the same grade level. The teacher should be prepared to comment on the originality of pieces she uses for examples. The children will pick up on your comments and start to experiment with other children's ideas while giving them their own slant.

Some people think this is copying. It really isn't. Anything that helps them start writing is an asset. Also, it is tremendously satisfying to an individual when the whole class likes his writing idea and decides to do something similar to it. There's an old saying. "Imitation is the sincerest form of flattery." I think that holds true here.

Give children functional, real-world writing assignments to facilitate temporary spelling.

For example: After we had visited a first-grade classroom for a play, I had one of my students write a thank-you note. Much to her delight the first-grade teacher wrote back complimenting her on her writing.

Students also can be encouraged to write invitations, requests, lists, messages, and questions to which you will respond. (See Figure 38).

Encourage temporary spelling by helping children learn the alphabet, giving them lots of writing experiences, and surrounding them with print. Allow them to compare and categorize words in various ways.

But whatever you do, don't give them the spelling. Make them use their best spelling strategies to figure it out by themselves.

Don't give up! It takes some classes longer to get into the sync of temporary spelling than others. One first-grade teacher told me his class (which had not experienced a developmentally appropriate kindergarten-writing program) took six weeks to feel confident and free about writing using temporary spelling.

When you are tempted to dump the whole idea, review the values of temporary spelling and reinspire yourself. Persevere! The results will be well worth your efforts.

Question: What do I do with the child who could write using temporary spelling but refuses because "it takes too long" ?

Answer: When this happened in my classroom, I would firmly challenge the child to "try." Usually after one challenge, the child would get so excited about what she had accomplished that she would continue to write using temporary spelling with no more prods.

But there are exceptions to every rule. If a child is capable of temporary spelling but prefers to use drawings and scribbles, there may not be much you can do. I had a child like this, and with gritted teeth I allowed him to pick his own writing method, constantly feeling guilty that I should be pushing him harder. Eventually he progressed to first grade, and much to my surprise, turned into an accomplished, creative writer. While he was in fourth grade his mother told me he wanted to become a writer. He's now in high school, works on the school news-paper, and is a highly motivated and articulate writer. I wonder what would have happened if I had really gotten on his case. The way it turned out, I guess I did the right thing. In cases like this, use your common sense, then observe the results for future reference.

Question: What about the child who is so caught up with "correct" spelling that she refuses to use temporary spelling?

Answer: I review this with my class many times. I tell them to get their thoughts down, and use temporary spelling for now. I say if they are unsure of a spelling, to give it their best shot, then circle it and go on. If they're paging through a dictionary, or coming up to my desk asking for the spelling, they are going to lose their chain of thought and their very important message.

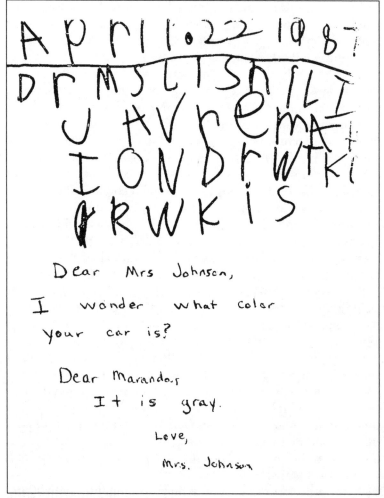

APril 22 1987

DR MSLTSnILI
UAVReMAt
IONDrWtKi
RWKIS

Dear Mrs Johnson,

I wonder what color
your car is?

Dear Marandas
    It is gray.

        Love,
        Mrs. Johnson

Figure 38: The child uses journal writing to ask the teacher a
question.

Many times children who are obsessed with perfect spelling settle into the safe routine. They use only words they can spell. You can imagine what this does to the quality of their writing. It becomes very mundane and lacks the freshness of the child who creates spellings freely and joyfully.

A teacher friend of mine had a problem with a student who refused to write anything but correct spelling. She talked, cajoled, wheedled, and ordered, but it was all to no avail. I suggested that she have a conference with the boy's parents and find out if he was getting pressure from home. She met with the parents, and suddenly the boy started to write freely.

I had a similar experience with one of my daughter's college roommates. When one of Penny's boys started to experience a developmentally appropriate writing classroom, she was horrified. He wasn't spelling correctly. Wouldn't that ruin him for life? My daughter asked me to send Penny the self-published version of this book. After reading the chapters on temporary spelling, Penny not only wrote me, she also called me. She was so relieved and happy that her son was in a class where the teacher was doing such a good job!

Question: Are there any children who do temporary spelling spontaneously?

Answer: Yes, but very few. Usually children have to be introduced to temporary spelling. Sometimes temporary spelling begins when the teacher gives the children permission to use it!

Question: What does the research say about children who use temporary spelling spontaneously?

Answer: They all had parents who were willing to accept the child's spelling efforts, provide materials for writing, and answer questions. The quality of the adult response to their child's questions and spelling attempts seemed to be of great importance in encouraging temporary spelling. Other things these children had in common were a wide range of experience involving the written language and its uses. This seemed to highly motivate them to write.

Question: Won't temporary spelling interfere with conventional spelling?

Answer: No. Temporary spelling errors do not interfere with learning to spell. These errors can be compared to a child's early attempts to walk, talk, and draw. We don't panic over the first phonemes a child utters, worrying that his "goo-goo" may become a pattern of his speech development for life. We don't get dismayed that the child's first steps aren't exactly steady, and we don't expect the child's first drawing to be a Rembrandt.

Why then do we expect the child's first spelling efforts to be perfect, and why do we make them feel like second-class citizens when they don't produce the correct spelling on their first tries?

No wonder children get turned off to writing. If we treated children's walking, speaking, and drawing the way we do their spelling, I doubt they would ever walk, talk, or draw....at least not normally.

These initial attempts at spelling are not bad habits that must be overcome. The temporary speller seldom uses the same spelling twice. Natural classroom pressures move the temporary speller toward correctness. As the child develops academically by seeing, hearing, and using more words, spelling improves.

Writing experience seems to be vitally beneficial to the student's future spelling success. Children who are in the habit of writing copious amounts will begin to incorporate traditional spelling and mechanics into their writing.

Early temporary spellers learn and spell more readily than students who do not attempt to write before learning to read. This early learning occurs because temporary spelling focuses the child's attentions on specific details of words, letters, sounds, and sequence of letters. This awareness probably contributes to accuracy of visually inspecting words while reading and also enhances accurate visual memory of word forms. Both are essential to spelling competency.

Set... Writing Strategies

Every child can write. It is up to the teacher to provide a broad range of writing strategies capable of unlocking the writing talent in each student.

Children learn to write by writing. All the strategies in this section challenge the gifted to higher levels of excellence, but they also affirm the not-so-gifted.

Many teachers know the values, stages, and rules of writing, but they are unsure where to begin.
This section is for them.

First steps are very important. To get you going, I detail step-by-step instructions for developmentally appropriate strategies that can be used successfully with young children. I will also give helpful hints to expedite these procedures, and I will propose a tentative time schedule for introduction of these strategies.

The following writing strategies (Chapters 6-15) can be used in a literature-based setting, or with any readiness series. Use your readiness materials to introduce the letters and sounds, but reinforce these skills through writing instead of using the traditional workbooks and runoffs.

Drawing by Jacob
Kindergarten Student

Chapter 6

Individual Language-Experience Story (ILES)

Drawing by Kimberley, Kindergarten Student

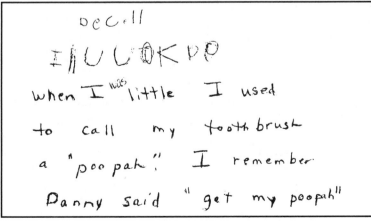

Drawing by Stacy, Kindergarten Student

One of the first articles I read on early-childhood writing said that the group language-experience story was the way to lead children into early writing experiences.

Most teachers are aware of language-experience stories. They follow this format: Your class has some kind of experience, a field trip, for example. When you return from the field trip, you gather the children around you. You point to a large sheet of white paper and show them you have a marker. You then explain to them that they are going to write a story about their trip. The children, one at a time, contribute wonderful sentences that describe their adventures. While they are dictating these sentences to the teacher, who is busily writing them on a large sheet of paper, the rest of the class sits quietly and attentively listens until it's their turn to speak. After the story is written, the teacher reads it to the class. Next the class reads it with the teacher, then by themselves.

Does this sound as if it would work?

It certainly didn't in my kindergarten classroom!

With an extremely verbal class plus several severe behavior problems, you can imagine what happened. Have you ever heard a shouting match among kindergarten children that is completely out of control? They all wanted to contribute at the same time.

That's what happened when I first tried the language-experience story. I met with complete failure. I was ready to pitch the whole strategy until I reviewed its benefits.

The language-experience story teaches children that their spoken ideas can be put into written form. Children become aware of letters, sounds, punctuation, word forms, sentence structures, etc. while writing these stories. The discussion that precedes the writing benefits the children because it stimulates clearer understanding of what they are writing about. When language experience is done correctly, children zero in on all the skills of reading because the skills are taught from the children's own words. Learning gained through this experience becomes very meaningful to young students.

Every education major knows that meaningful learning is more readily retained and understood.

I decided that I needed to keep the language-experience story because of its many benefits, but how was I going to manage it so it didn't turn into chaos?

I decided to shift the emphasis from the *group* to the *individual* and call it the Individual Language-Experience Story, hereafter referred to as ILES.

This strategy is unique in that it can be accomplished in five minutes, (right after sharing time), or your class can spend as much as half an hour on it.

ILES is very simple. The first day of school tell your students that they're all going to write a piece every day. Reassure them by telling them that they will say the words out loud that they want written, and that you will write these on a large tablet. But it will still be their pieces.

Model the procedure by writing a short story yourself. (Two or three sentences is fine.) Also model the different types of narrative: an expository piece and a fictional story. If you only model one type of writing, your class will think it has to write that type all year. But if you model both, you show them they have a choice.

At the beginning of the year, I ask an extremely verbal child to model the first one. After that, I use a class list that I hang next to my large tablet. If a child wants to pass when it's his turn, he has that right. Usually by the third time through the list of names everyone wants to write because it is a big deal to them.

Why is it a big deal? The author-for-the-day gets to make up the piece by herself, and everyone else has to listen. She gets to answer questions about the piece, and she gets to use the pointer to point to certain things in her piece. She wears an Author badge all day. She gets certain privileges if she is the author. (You could make her the leader for that day, for example). Her writing will be displayed for all to see. At the end of the day, she takes her writing home to share with her family. She chooses people from the class to find the new letter, or to identify any skill that the class has been studying.

All these little choices give kids the feeling that they have power, which they love. The thing they don't realize is that the power is controlled very easily by the teacher.

After the child is chosen to be the author he moves to the Author Chair. The teacher asks, "What color of marker should I use?" The child indicates his choice. The teacher then writes across the top of the tablet, speaking as she writes, "Written by," and adds the child's name and the date.

Then comes the waiting game. The child will say something like this: "I went to my grandma's last night."

The teacher waits until he has dictated one sentence, then stops him. The teacher turns to the class and asks, "What did he say?" The class responds, "I went to my grandma's last night." The teacher then writes it on the tablet in big letters, saying the words as she writes them. She exaggerates spaces between the words and enlarges the punctuation. When she finishes, she turns back to the author and says, "Go on." The child dictates another sentence, following the same procedure.

The teacher should never turn to the class to ask for its response until after the child dictates a complete sentence. Some teachers write down one word at a time. This is not a terrible practice, but it makes it tough for the class to follow. It is better to teach the kids to think in complete thoughts. By waiting until the child dictates a complete sentence, I am covertly teaching the concept of "sentence."

To keep this strategy short, *write big!* Then when you get to the end of the page, say, "Oops, we have to stop." If they say they have more to say—and some will—write Chapter 1 on top of the page. Then suggest to them that they can write Chapter 2 when they get home. (I found out later that my class picked up the sounds for "ch" from this practice!)

When the child is finished, the teacher takes a pointer (which the child has chosen), and after inviting the class to read with her, reads the child's words.

It is important to have a pointer! I have all kinds: a magic wand, a large pencil, an antenna. If you don't have one, use a yardstick.

The teacher should model pointing at the text of the child's message in a non-jerky manner. Don't pause between each word. We want kids to read fluently in phrases. The stop-and-go reading that results from pointing at each word will not enhance your student's fluency.

After the teacher reads the story with the class, she invites the child to lead the class in the reading and pointing. The teacher may have to help with this at first, but they seem to pick it up very swiftly.

After the second reading, the class may ask three questions about the story. The author gets to choose whose question he will answer. If someone wants to ask a question, he raises his hand and waits to be recognized by the author. The author is in total control, and amazingly, the class respects this control. If you want to make this strategy last longer you can let more children ask questions.

The questioning aspect of the ILES is actually setting the stage for future editing. Through the questioning process young authors find out that there are lots of other details they could have written to make their messages more interesting and more understandable.

After the questioning period, the author sits down in the group again, and the teacher takes over. The teacher can introduce, reinforce, and teach skills at this time.

Excuse Me, I Have A Question

Question: How do you get kids started doing the ILES?

Answer: The ILES is very interesting to young writers. Motivating your students is not a problem. They will beg to do it every day and will remind you if you have forgotten. Getting them this excited about something that is teaching them so many skills with their own words brings gladness to a teacher's heart.

Question: What does the ILES do for your student's self-esteem?

Answer: Not only are the child's skills and concepts enhanced by this strategy, self-worth grows as the child dictates his message and leads the class in the reading. Fielding the questions that arise about his story is a public-speaking skill. The author has to think on his feet. Self-esteem is also enhanced because everyone has success with this strategy. The child cannot fail. The ILES is an automatic entry into writing competence.

Question: What are some skills that a kindergarten teacher could introduce, teach, and reinforce during ILES?

Answer: punctuation
   spacing
   complete sentences
   phonics
   left-to-right progression
   correct spelling
   title and main idea
   capitalization
   concept of author
   choral reading
   word identification
   recall (auditory memory and sequence)
   cloze procedure (Cover words of story with post-a-notes.
      See if children can identify hidden words.)
   Locate words that start with the same letter or vowel
      sounds.
   comprehension skills: predict what will happen next
   class word banks
   Dramatize the story.
   beginning and ending sounds
   rhyming words
   reading aloud as a group or singly
   blend and digraph recognition
   questioning skills
   Is the story fact or fiction?
   Count words, sentences, paragraphs.

How many lines, how many sentences?
Teacher models good letter formation.
Class learns names of students.
color words
names of months and days of week
abbreviations
words with double letters

You will find many occasions to teach other skills and concepts, which aren't even mentioned above, from the ILES writings.

Keep track of all the skills you teach during ILES. Then at the end of the year, you will find you have covered all the material your curriculum guide requires. You'll be shocked by all the skills you taught that were several grade levels above yours.

I'm not suggesting that you expect your students to have complete mastery of advanced concepts, but if a good example occurs in student writing (for example, if a student's sentence begins with an interjection), I would take advantage of the situation. In a low-key manner, the teacher could say, "This word is an interjection! There are two ways we could punctuate it."

Question: What do you do with the ILESs when you are through with them?

Answer: I had children take their stories home at the end of the day. I encourage them to finish these at home with their parents. If they wanted to bring the pieces back to school and read the new part, that was fine too.

You also can save them and publish a kindergarten newspaper every so often. The kids love to take these home and read them to their parents. Since they all read each other's writings as they're being written, they have a pretty good idea of the content. Their beginning phonics helps them sound out quite a few of the words. Helpful parents would be glad to help them read the rest.

Question: Do you do just one ILES per day?

Answer: This is up to the teacher. If the kids really respond to this writing strategy you may want to do two of these per day. I know teachers who did one right away in the morning and one after lunch. It depends on the length of your day. Observe your class response to the ILES, then make a decision regarding frequency.

Question: What if a child dictates a message that is grammatically incorrect?

Answer: I accept whatever they say. Do not allow anyone to criticize another's writing. The reason for this rule is obvious: the author must feel safe. If a perfectionist in the class decides to take potshots at every writing, kids will stop writing.

This is not to say that I don't do anything about their errors. For the child who is having difficulty coming up with complete sentences, for example, the fact that I don't start scribing his words until he has dictated a complete sentence gives some powerful indirect instruction to the child without making a big deal out of it. I will also work with that child on language development during center time.

Question: What happens if the child dictates a sentence that is inappropriate?

Answer: It has happened to me several times. Once a student dictated a message concerning a situation that was occurring at his home. It was immediately apparent that this student's message would not be healthy or instructive for the rest of the class. I stopped him mid-sentence and asked him quietly if I could see him in the hall. When we got to the privacy of the hall I was extremely low key. I told him this was probably not a message we should share with the whole class. I said he could talk to me privately about it, or, if he liked, I could send him to the guidance counselor, who was always a willing listener. I concluded by telling him that it might be wise to think about another topic for his ILES message.

I was afraid that we might have lots of questions when we re-entered the room, but the kids didn't catch what had happened because of the speed of our hasty exit. If you have a plan of action for a situation like this, you can get by without creating a scene that is poten-tially upsetting to your whole class.

Question: Do the children always dictate exciting stories?

Answer: No, they're usually rather bland and generic. But every so often someone will come up with a hilarious one, and these really lend themselves to class participation. The rest of the class love to read these, act them out, and illustrate them.

One very quiet child dictated the following story: "Last Sunday my cat fell in the toilet. We could not get him out. So my dad got him out. We had to use the blow comb to get him dry!"

By the time he finished dictating, I was laughing, and the class was laughing. Doctors and psychologists and theologians say we ought to laugh more for our health. I'm sure we were all healthier because of this boy's "dry" sense of humor that day.

Question: Could the ILES be used in remedial reading when it is appropriate?

Answer: Renae Groen, one of my second-grade-teacher colleagues, inherited a group of children one year who were totally defeated in learning to read. After trying several reading strategies that failed, Renae decide to try the ILES. She wrote an ILES with all her struggling students, and used their exact writings for her reading program.

Renae did all the things you usually do with the stories that you have your students read. She introduced vocabulary, she asked questions to encourage her students to predict outcomes, and she asked other questions that the children would be able to answer during guided silent reading.

The *cloze* method was employed to gain comprehension. This process removes every fifth or sixth word from the story. The removed words are placed at the bottom of the page in a mixed order. The children are directed to replace the words where they make sense.

Renae also pulled sentences from the stories and mixed their order. It was the students' job to replace the sentences in the correct sequence.

The author of the story got to lead the rest of the class in reading it orally. The stories were read again and again. Renae felt it even helped the rhythm of the children's reading.

Did using the ILES help these reluctant writers? I rode all the way to Rapid City, South Dakota, (a six-hour drive) with a grandmother who sang Renae's praises for quite a few of those miles. This grandmother felt that Renae's use of the ILES had led her grandchild back to loving reading.

Finally....

The ILES has many merits that enable your students to progress to new plateaus of meaningful language knowledge. It enhances your students' self-esteem because everyone is successful. It is easy and inexpensive to accomplish, and, best of all, your students will love doing it.

Chapter 7

Journal Writing

Figure 39: *The child uses journal writing when something important happens.*

Kindergarten and first-grade children's best writing will not originate in "cute story starters." The free-writing experience of journal writing is perhaps the most productive component in terms of language development and student interest in the early grades. When your students write in their journals *they write about what is important to them.*

In kindergarten start the journal writing in late November or early December. In first grade begin the first day. During journal writing encourage children to write something using whatever means they can devise. To help the children think of themselves as writers, the teacher never refers to their writing as a "scribble," "drawing," or "temporary spelling." Instead, the children are asked, "What have you written?" no matter what writing method they use.

Encourage table talk during their daily writing.

Instruct them to write only on one page. Encourage them to copy the date then proceed with their writing. *There are no assigned topics.* The children write about anything they choose.

What do young children write about when they have a choice? You can expect mostly writings about *reality.* Children first gravitate toward expository writing (See Figures 39, 40). These are the real happenings in a child's life concerning TV, family, peers, play experiences, emotions, fears, love, anger, and sadness. Some of their writings deal with *isolated ideas.* These writings include one or two sentences about a topic the child seems to pull out of the air, for example a descriptive prose passage one of my children wrote spontaneously (See Figure 41). The smallest group of journal entries are *fantasy stories.* (See Figures 42, 43, 44). Some years individual classes write more of this type of journal entry and find added joy when they can share them with each other, especially if they think these are funny.

The first year I tried journaling, I had the children bring to class regular spiral notebooks. I instructed them before writing to disregard the lines if they chose. After that, our school provided plain white-paper journals, with 70 or 80 pages, bound with black plastic binders by our super office staff. Some teachers use self-constructed five-day journals and send them home at the end of each week. I prefer a journal that will last a year. Having all of the children's journal writings in one book facilitates evaluation at the end of the year. It also becomes a treasured keepsake for parents.

How to Start Journaling With Your Class

In kindergarten I talk about journals for several weeks before we start in the actual journals. We even do a few practice pages. I demonstrate temporary spelling. I tell them that however they choose to write,

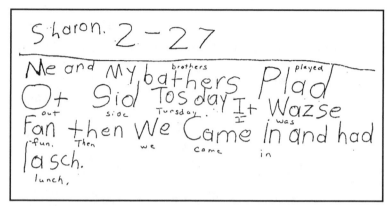

Figure 40: *The child uses journal writing to relate an ordinary, everyday incident.*

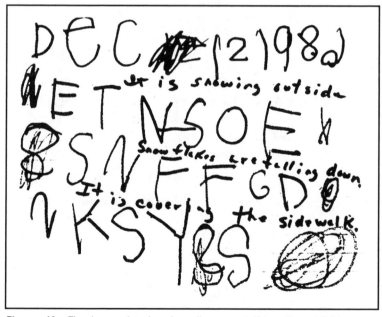

Figure 41: *The journal entry describes something the child has observed.*

Figure 42: *The child is using journal writing to express fantasy.*

Text within the drawing:

Jan. 6, 1985

A big snowflake is coming on the house and its gonna crash the houses

Figure 43: *The child imagines what would happen if a snowflake were enormous.*

Figure 44: *The child expresses fantasy as she draws and dictates in her journal.*

they will have to read it to me because just as they are unable to read my writing, sometimes I can't read theirs. They have to help me out.

You may have to follow this process in first grade too if your students haven't been in a kindergarten class using developmentally appropriate writing activities.

After you have introduced them to the journaling process, it's time to begin. Tell them the rules:

- Write on one page only.

- Copy the date on the top of the page.

- You may write about anything you wish.

- You may use your favorite writing instrument.

- Everyone stays in their desks for five minutes. When the timer goes off, if they are finished, they may bring their journal, open to their writing, to the teacher. (This will save you lots of time.) When they leave their journal with the teacher they pick up a low-profile activity page that will keep them occupied until everyone else is through. Children who are still writing may continue to write as long as they like. *They do not have to complete the activities the quick writers are working on.*

Set your timer for five minutes as the children begin to write. This is the time for you to model journal writing yourself.

Meet with children one at a time by pulling the bottom journal out of the stack and calling that child's name. When they come up to you, (They will stand very close.) ask them what they have written. Then write their words down in small letters, preferably at the bottom of the page. Meet with each student for one minute only — the conferences usually last less than one minute — then call the next child. (See the *Writing Conference* chapter.)

Journal writing takes 30 minutes if you have less than 20 pupils. To have a conference with more than 20 pupils, you will need help from, perhaps, a parent volunteer or a teacher's aide. Train these individuals to conduct conferences the same way you do. Ask them to relate any unusual messages to you.

Activities to Keep Kids Occupied After Journal Writing

The following is a list of activities I routinely use to keep kids occupied who have finished writing early. You will notice there are no wildly exciting jobs in this list, no computer games, and no playing with the class hamster. I purposely kept it low-profile. I wanted the children to value writing. I didn't want to de-emphasize its importance by providing activities that would encourage children to race through their writing.

1. writing center
2. reading center
3. cutting worksheets
4. coloring activities
5. tracing activities
6. writing ABCs or numerals
7. listening center with earphones
8. extra work-sheet box—children have a choice
9. puzzles
10. Laminate hidden-picture pages from *Highlights*. Let kids find hidden pictures with markers.
11. cut-and-paste activities
12. simple art projects
13. miscellaneous run-offs children can do by themselves (math, science, social studies)
14. color-by-number pictures
15. dot-to-dot activities
16. mazes
17. miscellaneous wipe-offs
18. cut pictures from magazines (*National Geographic* works great!)
19. Draw a picture.
20. Read or tell a story aloud softly to a stuffed animal or doll or another child.
21. Write your own words to laminated wordless books.

Finally,

Journal writing is a unique and satisfying experience for young children that increases kids' interest in writing. This method is popular and successful with the children probably because it makes them feel good about themselves. Feelings of competence grow as the children freely choose their own content and their own symbols to communicate their very worthwhile ideas (See Figures 47, 48, 49).

Teachers benefit from the journal-writing experience also. Through the writings you get to know the students better. During journal writing the children feel free to share their deepest thoughts and fondest dreams along with their secret fears and sorrows. (See Figures 45, 46, 50, 51, 52, 53). The fears and sorrows are alleviated a great deal by writing about them, or, in many cases you can reassure a student if you know his worries.

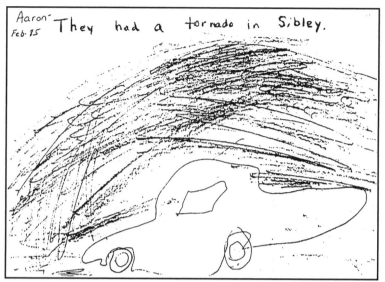

Figure 45: The child is using journal writing to express remembered fear.

Figure 46: The child is using journal writing to express emotions.

Figure 47: After a science unit, the child writes about a simple machine.

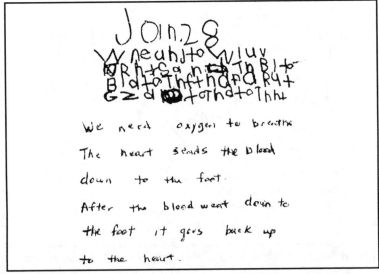

Figure 48: The child writes about her comprehension of the circulatory system.

APl - 14

ss·· is fn
Space   is   fun.

wSff
Reading is fun

ILKSL
I like school

is fto B Ln
Its fun to be learning

on
The end.

Figure 49: *The child responds in writing about a space unit.*

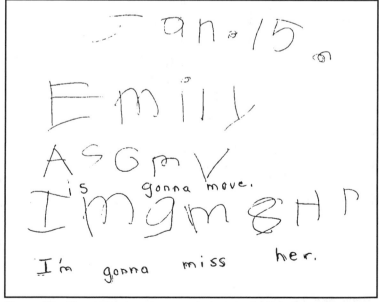

Jan.15.

EmIlY

ASGmV
is   gonna move.

Imgm8Hr
I'm gonna miss her.

Figure 50: *The writer is concerned about a friend who's moving.*

Figure 51: *The child tells about a bad dream.*

Figure 52: *The child expresses knowledge about war during the conference.*

Figure 53: The child communicates sorrow during the conference.

Chapter 8

The Writing Conference

Drawing by Mitchell Ackerman
Third Grade

The student-teacher writing conference is important in the K-1 writing experience. By meeting with beginning writers, the teacher plays a strategic role in the initial journal-writing experience.

The conferences ideally should occur right after the children have written in their journals. Follow this procedure:

- After a child completes his journal entry, he meets the teacher privately at a designated conferencing center.

- The teacher opens the journal and asks, "What have you written?" The teacher then proceeds to write the child's dictated remarks in the journal at the bottom of the page while he observes.

- The conference continues as the teacher makes some comment on the content of the child's writing. *This comment should in some way communicate to the child that what he has written is understood!*

Communicating Understanding

What statements or questions can a teacher voice to indicate understanding of the child's writings? Imagining a different comment for each child's writing would require rapid, creative thinking. I use some general guidelines to help me keep the experience new and fresh with each child:

- Simply restate or paraphrase the child's words.

- Question the child about some aspect of his writing. This could be an objective question that asks the child to clarify or explain an unclear part of his writing. (Example: "Where were you when this happened?" "When did this happen?")

- Ask, "How did this make you feel?"

- Inquire about what happened before and after the portrayed event.

- Quiz the child about what he liked best about his writing.

- Tell the child how his writing made you feel.

- Compliment some aspect of the child's writing sincerely. (Example: "You're the first one in the class to write words to a song!")

- Suggest a solution to a problem, comfort the child, straighten out a misunderstanding, or meet the student's needs in some other way.

Benefits of the Conference

Conferences are time consuming and a lot of work, but the benefits are impressive.

Of course, the chief aim of conferencing is to set the stage for revision and editing. It prepares the ground for later rewriting because the answers to the questions posed indicate that more details could have been shared.

The writing conference encourages and reinforces the writing experience. It supplies the child with an interested and caring audience.

The child's self-esteem is enhanced by the conference. Children love the conference because each day they can plan on a special time alone, eyeball-to-eyeball, with a listening teacher who really hears what they say as they share their thoughts and concerns. The conference can also act as a safety valve to enable children to vent problems they might be unable to verbalize without the one-on-one teacher contact.

The traditional show-and-tell time is supposed to be the time for this type of communication, but I find children write things they would never share with the class during show-and-tell time. (Not necessarily family secrets, but usually very ordinary fears, sorrows, and worries that concern the child.)

There's something about the intimacy of the conference appointment that opens communication channels for young children. Some shy children were barely able to say a word during our regular show-and-tell time, but their writings poured out worries and concerns that I was unaware of. "My grandpa is in the hospital," "My dog died," "We had a tornado," "He fell into a dark hole and couldn't get out," "My mom is sick," are but a few of the real concerns young children share during the conference.

The writing conference is of value to the teacher because the guilt that haunts you ("Did I touch base with that certain child today? Yesterday? Or this week?") is completely dispelled! The student-teacher writing conference leaves the teacher with a well-earned feeling of satisfaction. You meet the individual child's needs because you talk to each child one-on-one each day. While those meetings take place you respond to their real needs.

The teacher comes to know the child *very well* as a result of this conference. I think most teachers would agree that this knowledge about the child is tremendously beneficial for individualizing learning and assessing capabilities.

Conferences keep you sharp while listening to your student's dictation. I wish I could say that every student every day is going to write something wildly exciting, but that is not true. There may be several days or weeks when the ideas expressed may all seem rather mediocre, but don't give up. Even the mediocre thoughts deserve recognition because the child has still put effort and thought into forming them. Force yourself to think about what the child is trying to communicate. Don't just write their words down without thinking. Use that time to zero in on the message that child is sending you. Be prepared to be surprised about what you would have missed without that appointment.

Chapter 9

Draw and Write

Drawing by Maria Kramer
Third Grade

The relationship between drawing and writing always will be close. Drawing enhances children's abilities to organize their thoughts, helps them decide what to write, and enables them to remember details they might have forgotten.

First, have the children draw a picture depicting a subject the class has studied. (I use this strategy about once a month when we finish a teaching unit. It is an excellent way to bring closure and find out exactly what your students have learned.) Use large pages of story paper (12"x18"), which are blank on top and have lines on the bottom.

The Draw-and-Write strategy introduces children to four levels of entry into the writing experience. The following descriptions will help you identify students' current and progressive writing levels.

Children at Level One have small knowledge of the alphabet and little ability to form letters. These children dictate their information to teachers (or students—third grade or older), and watch them transcribe it. Even though they are unable to print, they start to realize and internalize information about printed language, and show creativity and quality ideas.

Children at Level Two dictate their ideas the same as Level One children do, but as soon as they finish the dictation, the children take colored markers and trace over the words and punctuation in their writing. (See Figure 54). The tracing is useful for many reasons, but especially so because the children are tracing their own words.

Children at Level Three dictate their message but the teacher or helper scribes the words on every other line. After the child has finished

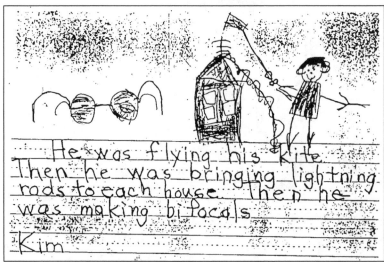

Figure 54: Example of writing using Draw-and-Write method. Child is at Stage Two, tracing.

dictating, he copies the teacher's words on the line below using colored markers. (See Figure 55). Copying is a tougher skill than tracing, and some kids won't be able to handle this.

Children at Level Four write on their own using temporary spelling. (See Figure 56). Risk taking and experimentation are essential at this level. After they finish, they trace over their temporary spelling with colored markers. Children at Level Four seem to write shorter pieces than children at Levels One, Two, and Three. Their finished products take more time, but their positive feelings about working independently overshadow any negative feelings about the time factor.

After the teacher transcribes their writing, Level One students read their pieces to the teacher, who then comments on content.

After Levels Two, Three, and Four finish their tracing and copying, they bring their writing to the teacher and read it as best they can. The teacher gives help as needed with the oral reading and comments on content.

I had total class participation using this method. The children felt happy about their pieces no matter what writing method they used. Drawing the pictures first seems to help the children focus their thoughts and actually enhances their ability to create written pieces.

Because most children had to draw, dictate, or write, and then trace, this writing strategy can easily take as much as thirty minutes, and that's not counting the oral reading time. To expedite the process, you will need plenty of help: either parent volunteers or older students.

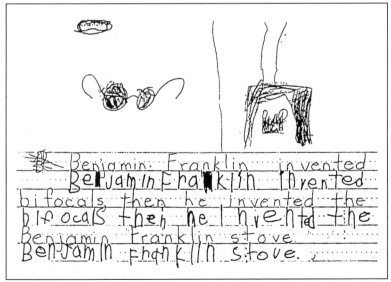

Figure 55: *Draw-and-Write, Level 3*

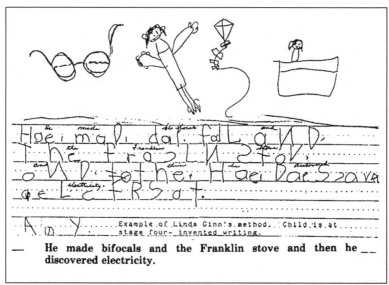

Figure 56: *Example of Draw-and-Write method. Child is at Stage Four, invented writing.*

But all the work is worth it. These writings with their interesting illustrations look great to administrators and children themselves. They are excellent for parent-night presentations.

An obvious advantage of this teaching method is that children can enter any of the four levels that best meets their current ability. Children are accepted wherever they are developmentally. This enhances positive feelings about themselves and writing.

Creating informational articles is important in education. Composing these kind of pieces forms the basis for later report writing.

I used the Draw-and-Write strategy after I had finished social studies, science, math, music, and P.E. units.

Using writing (which is reading also because children read as they write) definitely enhances the child's understanding of that particular content area. Writing reveals unclear areas of understanding that need to be re-taught. Using writing this way keeps teachers on track by forcing you to teach writing not as an independent skill but as a part of a whole, a very worthwhile concept for the beginning writer to understand.

Questions

Question: Why use the Draw-and-Write Strategy?

Answer: The students in your class who will shine at Draw and Write are the kids who enjoy making detailed drawings. Very often the quiet kids who didn't have much to contribute to class discussions will excel in the Draw-and-Write strategy.

This strategy seems to inspire students who normally can't think of a writing topic. The process of making the drawing leads them quite naturally into the writing. The major battle regarding what to write is already won. Studying the details of a drawing reacquaints the student with particulars they may have forgotten. If you allow children to draw before they write, they generate more words, display more fluency, and show greater syntactic maturity than other children who did not draw or who just colored a pre-drawn picture pertaining to a subject.

Question: What do you do with the Draw and Writes after they are finished?

Answer: They are displayed in the hall, then bound into a class book. At the end of the year, the books are dismantled, and each child's writing is placed in a personal writing folder.

Question: Is it important to date all the Draw and Writes?

Answer: Yes. This will help you note each child's writing progress.

Question: Do you need to train older students to help with this strategy?

Answer: Yes. Make sure they understand that they should not start writing until the child has dictated a whole sentence. (No one-word-at-a-time dictation).Tell them to print very legibly, to exaggerate spaces between words, and to exaggerate punctuation. After they finish, they should read the writing again with the student, encouraging her to read as much as possible.

If a kindergarten student is acting in an inappropriate manner, the older child or helper should be instructed to get the teacher. Some young writers will not be able to handle writing with an older student.

Question: What if the child won't dictate anything? What do you do?

Answer: I've had this frustrating experience happen a few times. Questioning them about the drawing usually frees their writer's block.

For someone who is absolutely stuck, make a completely ridiculous statement about their drawing. (For instance, if they have drawn a picture of an apple orchard, say "I see you've drawn an elephant here.") Of course they have to correct you, so the words will come pouring out then.

Question: What about parents who say, "I see all of the other writings (Levels One, Two, and Three) are all correctly spelled. Why has my child's writing got so many misspelled words?"

Answer: Explain about the four levels the children use with this strategy. Tell them their child is at a more advanced stage and doing great. Explain that the perfectly spelled writings were spelled by teachers and helpers, but their child worked out all his spellings on his own, a much harder job.

Question: Do you read these writings to the whole class?

Answer: Yes. After all the children are done I hold each writing up, let the class see the picture, and read the dictated words using my finger as a pointer. This is a highly engrossing activity because kids are very interested in the writings of others.

Question: Which level do I begin my children at?

Answer: I started all my kindergarten students at Level Two. If that is too hard for some, you will know right away. But most kindergarten children can trace. Keep an eye on them when they first do this. You can tell a lot about their development by one writing experience. First grade should probably start out at Level Three, and then be observed.

Chapter 10

Pattern Stories

Drawing by Jeff Kreiger
Second Grade

Pattern stories are an exciting way of linking writing with reading. The pattern books are based on familiar tales the kids know and love. Pattern stories are also known as "innovation" because the child is allowed to innovate or be creative with certain aspects of the story. Suddenly a whole new story emerges that contains the child's ideas.

Pattern stories are a legitimate form of writing. They allow the writer to borrow the story structure, characters, setting, etc., and then change them. This is okay to do. It is not against the law. One mother was concerned because one of her sons wrote highly creative original stories, while her other son wrote innovations. I reassured her that both were acceptable, and that the son who wrote innovations was being creative in his own way.

It is very interesting to see what happens when a small change is made in the characters, setting, or names in a story. The whole tone of the story changes. It seems like a brand new story. For instance, a pattern story can be written on the all-time favorite of kids, *Miss Nelson is Missing*. Start out by reading the story several times to your class. Then let the class rename the teacher. (Don't be surprised if they put your name in the slot!) Next, ask the kids questions: "What are some things that kids do in school that could get them in trouble?" Insert the suggested changes into the actual book with sticky notes. Then change the room number of Miss Nelson's room. Keep going in this vein until you get through the whole book. Then write the words on the plain white sheets and invite children to make accompanying illustrations. The illustrations could be pasted above the words when the kids are happy with their drawings. (You save yourself lots of work by doing it this way.)

How about the *Curious George* books? Every child seems to love them. Have your class write an innovation on the *Curious George* stories. First, discuss the structure of all *Curious George* books. Write the kids' observations on the board:

1) Curious George and the Man With the Yellow Hat go somewhere or do something.

2) The Man With the Yellow Hat tells George to stay out of trouble.

3) George doesn't obey TMWTYH and gets in trouble.

4) Even though he's in trouble, he suddenly becomes a hero.

   Now pull out a *Curious George* book, let the kids change a few things, and *voila!*, a brand new book.

The Nitty-Gritty Facts about Writing Pattern Stories

Sound like fun? It is. Reading the stories, making up the innovations, then illustrating these are tremendously engaging activities for children, so there isn't much need for a great amount of teacher motivation.

There are five ways the pattern books can be utilized by your class:

1) Use the book with the original text. Have your students draw different pictures.

   Bill Martin's *Brown Bear, Brown Bear* is perfect for this. Assign one illustration to each child. On the page where you see children, place a picture of your whole class. On the page where you see the mother, change it to "teacher" and use your picture.

2) Copy pictures out of the original story, but change the text in various ways.

   Joy Cowley's much-loved *Mrs. Wishy-Washy* works well for this one. Use the pictures but change the words. Do this in front of the class using sticky notes to change the original text. Change Mrs. Wishy-Washy's name. Instead of the animals saying, "Oh, lovely mud!", have your class come up with different words like, "Oh, sloppy goop!"

   Then have students try to match the original drawings, put the new text on the pages and you have a new book.

3) Use the structure established by the original book, but change the situation.

   I use the book *My Mom Travels a Lot* by C. F. Bauer for this one. This story is written from a child's viewpoint giving the advantages and disadvantages of having a traveling mother. The text goes something like this: "My mom travels a lot. That's good because we get to take her to the airport. That's bad because we don't get Mom's good-night kisses. That's good because Dad lets us eat out a lot. That's bad because we don't get Mom's homemade lasagna," etc.

   Use this concept to have your class write about the good and bad of any subject. If you're having several rainy days in a row, write a story about the pros and cons of rainy days. Start out by asking who would like to draw a picture of a rainy day. Someone volunteers. Write "It was a Rainy Day." across the top of a large white sheet of construction paper. Give it to the child who volunteered. He goes to his table to get started. Then ask, "What's good about a rainy day?" Someone says, "The grass grows." Write "That's good because the grass grows." across the top of the next sheet. Ask who would like to draw a picture to go with this text. Give it to the volunteer who goes back to his desk to get to work. Then say, "What's bad about the rainy day?" Take a suggestion and write it on the next sheet, ask for a volunteer, etc. Keep up this procedure until everyone has a page to do. Don't forget to have someone make a cover.

If you have three people left who are trying to come up with another idea, and they can't think of any, ask the children who are working at their desks for suggestions.

4) Change the text and the pictures.

Again, Bill Martin's book *Brown Bear, Brown Bear* is perfect for this one. At the beginning of the year, I want my students to know each other's names and faces. Have each child construct one page of a new class pattern book titled *People, People*.

I photocopy pages with the following written in large print:

"_____, _____, what do you see?"

"I see _____ looking at me."

Instruct the kids to write their names in the first two blanks, then trace all the letters with colored markers. (You might want to cover the bottom blanks with sticky notes so they don't get confused and fill that one in too.) You fill in the bottom blank as you assemble the book. The person who is on the next page will have her name in the bottom blank.

We ended the book with a picture of the whole class. Of course, you must have a page for the teacher. It wouldn't hurt to include all the adults the children come in contact with at school, such as other teachers, the principal, the secretary, the custodian, the assistants, lunch workers, etc.

Another innovation that works with *Brown Bear, Brown Bear* was shared with me by Yvonne Sieve, a first-grade teacher. After her students complete a social studies unit on occupations, they write the following book complete with illustrations.

Occupations

Written by Mrs. Sieve's Creative First -Grade Class

Taxi driver, taxi driver, what do you do?
I drive taxi for people like you.
Baker, baker, what do you do?
I bake bread and donuts for people like you.
etc.

At the end of the poem, Yvonne listed all her students' names and what they wanted to be when they grew up.

5) Have the child construct books using the same text and pictures. *Mrs. Wishy Washy* works well for this writing. More advanced students can copy the words, and less skilled children can help with the illustrations.

Your Final Instructions Are....

Remember to give credit to the title, author, and illustrator of the original book on the cover page of your class pattern book.

There is a list of pattern stories at the end of this book, but actually you can make any story into a pattern story with a little creativity.

Students love making pattern books, and they especially love reading them later. I had parent volunteers come to my room and read with my students. Guess which books my students requested the most? Their own pattern books.

Why? There are several good reasons.

They *made* these books. They feel like the creators and authors. They are justifiably proud and want to show them off. We're talking about ownership of the writing process.

They are easy to read, not just because the words are simple, but because my students are part of the process of creation, and this leads to word-identification skills beyond their age levels.

The pattern books are entertaining. No matter how many times the pattern books are read, the kids still are fascinated by the words and illustrations made by members of their own class.

Chapter 11

The Class Mascot and Journal Writing

Snowball Whiskers goes home with each child.

What does a teddy bear have to do with a kindergarten writing program? I found this idea suggested for first-grade children, but it seemed so intriguing that I decided to take a chance and try it with my kindergarten class.

Shortly after Christmas I purchased a K-MART Teddy Bear. (It doesn't have to be a bear. With head lice an ever-present threat, I would recommend something that could be washed completely — say, a rubber doll or animal.)

Right after Christmas seems to be a good time to begin the Mascot Writing Experience. There is usually a downtime after all the holiday excitement. Most teachers search for special activities to pique student interest again. Introduce your class mascot and see how they react!

Tell the class that you have adopted a teddy bear (or whatever), and that you wondered if they would help you take care of it. Clearly make it their choice to help. Ask who is interested. They will all raise their hands. Stress the responsibilities involved in the care of the teddy. Tell them that each child will have to take the teddy home and care for him overnight.

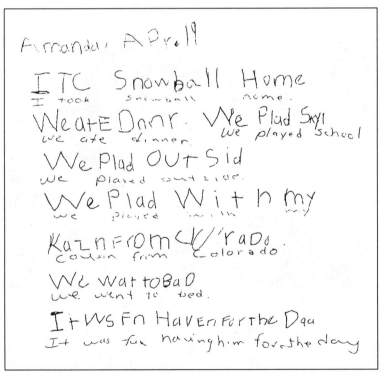

April 19 entry in Snowball's journal.

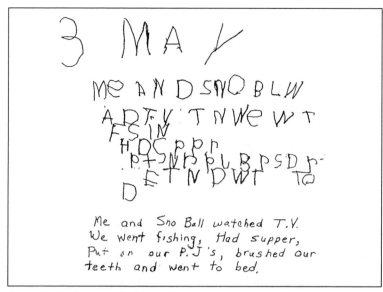

An entry in Snowball's journal.

An entry in Snowball's journal.

May 19 Danele

me and
Snowball
Went
to Shelbon.
It was raining
and It hailed.
Snowball got
Mared ~married.
We had a fun Day.

Snowball's journal entry.

I said I would provide the bear with a small suitcase that contained his everyday clothes, pajamas, toothbrush, blanket, and notebook. I told them to put on his pajamas at bedtime and pretend to brush his teeth. I said to make sure he was tucked under his blanket before he went to sleep because "he couldn't sleep without his blanket," a fact they all seemed to identify with. Of course, they would have to get him dressed again the next morning.

Tell the children they need to help name the bear. After they suggest several names, vote. The names "Snowball" and "Whiskers" tied, so we compromised and named the bear "Snowball Whiskers."

Notice how the temporary spelling improves as the year progresses.

Then direct the children's attention to the journal in the suitcase. (I had purchased a spiral notebook with a bear's picture on the cover.) By this time of year your students are writing in their own journals and are familiar with the routine of writing the date on each page and only using one page for each entry. Tell them you want them to write in the mascot's journal every day, using temporary spelling (not scribbles or drawings. Or you can decide to have them dictate and their parents write. It is up to you.) They should relate activities they experience while the mascot is at their house. Inform them that children who take the mascot home will read what they have written in the journal the next school day during sharing time.

Snowball had an active sports life along with his many other activities. A well-rounded bear.

Post the following letter inside the cover of the mascot's journal to give the parents direction if help is needed.

Dear Parents,

Our class has adopted this (teddy bear). The children are responsible for taking him home and bringing him back the following day. His stocking cap should remain on at all times, but his scarf may be removed when his pajamas are put on. This suitcase contains his pajamas, toothbrush, blanket, and journal. THIS IS WHERE YOU COME IN.

Direct the children to write on ONE page of the journal at night before going to bed. They should write as best they can what they and the teddy did that afternoon and evening (activities, food, TV, etc.).

Assist the children by helping them remember their activities. Pronounce the words slowly, and let them spell the words as best they can. Don't help them spell; make them come up with the sounds. Once they have written a letter, let it stand. Don't expect perfect spelling or spacing. Accept their ideas on spelling.

When they finish, read it again with them and make small notes by their writing if a word is unreadable. For example, IATSPR (child's writing) might be noted as "I ate supper."

Each day the child will share this journal writing with the whole class. The children are very excited about this experience. I know it will be helpful to them in more ways than they know.

Thank you for participating in your child's writing experience.

Mrs. Johnson

Make sure the first child who writes in the mascot's journal follows these instructions perfectly. Talk to the first parent involved so they realize the importance of allowing temporary spelling. I found the first writing is the model for all that follow. If you have a parent who spells every word perfectly for the child, all the other parents will follow suit.

The parents generally did a good job of following my guidelines. The bear turned out to have a highly successful social life. He went shopping frequently, rode a bike, went on vacations, went skiing, had his picture taken with my students (see picture at beginning of chapter), got married! and went out for pizza often.

I knew my students were excited about the mascot, but I didn't know how much this excitement transferred to their homes. One night my husband and I were shopping in a large department store when a shopping cart came rolling up beside me. Our class mascot was sitting in the infant seat in the cart. Pushing the cart was one of my students. Her dad stood a short distance away watching my surprised reaction. He said they had just come from a pizza restaurant and that the mascot had sat in a high chair there while the family ate supper!

How did this experience benefit my students? What did adopting a class mascot do for the whole class?

It was an obvious incentive for my students to write outside of class using the letters and sounds they were learning. (See selected journal entries.)

The experience gave me an opening to talk about parenting skills. Before you send the mascot home, have your class discuss how to treat him and how to keep him clean. I don't think it is ever too early to talk about the responsibilities of caretaking. Our mascot provided a natural opening into the subject.

The temporary spelling in the journal involves the students' parents in the writing process. I want the parents to see what their children are learning about sound-symbol relationships. The child's letter-and-sound knowledge becomes evident while the parent watches and supervises the journal entries. I am also aware of the important suggestions, reinforcement, and encouragement the parents provide as they assist the child write so painstakingly in the journal.

Taking care of the mascot enhances a child's sense of responsibility. The children have a lot to remember. They arrive each day laden with suitcase, mascot (in a plastic shopping bag), and their bookbags. If they forgot to change him out of his pajamas, the other children ask why. This is rather embarrassing and usually won't happen twice.

I was worried about losing the supplies kept in the suitcase, but this was not a problem. You will find as the year progresses that many things will be added as the children and their families contribute clothing, toys, books, and special gifts for the mascot.

The mascot will stimulate your students' imaginations. One of the most delightful parts of childhood is imaginative play. Too often with the pressures of teaching the required curriculum, we forget about exciting the child's imaginative processes. That is sad. In kindergarten and first grade we teach our students to differentiate between fiction and non-fiction, but we very seldom let them write examples of both.

A class mascot helps your students accomplish imaginative story telling. Model this for them in the beginning, then watch then take off. Every day as the children write in the journal, they imagine the mascot doing all the things they are doing. You can see by the journal pages I include in this chapter that they had a lot of fun with a very ordinary teddy bear. It seems to me their imaginative thoughts grow more vivid as the year progresses.

Your class will even insist on having a birthday party for your mascot. Democratic procedure will determine the date of the birthday. Have one of the kids take the mascot out in the hall while you are planning the party so it will be a surprise! Purchase special party hats, ask someone to contribute a cake, have each child construct a birthday card (another real writing experience), and sing the birthday song. Your class will enjoy this occasion as much as a real child's party.

The children learn to express love by this experience. Is it important to have someone to love? Is it important to have someone love you? Of course it is. The children's comments and their journal entries lead you to believe they love the mascot dearly. They also believe that he loves them too.

The love that was felt for the mascot becomes so vivid that the children start to think of him as a real person. By the end of the school year, they wonder rather tearfully, what is going to become of the mascot? We discuss the various options and make a group decision. One year we drew names and the mascot went home with the winner. Another year they elected to leave him with me, so they could visit him "whenever they wanted." I'll leave this to your discretion.

Adopt a Class Mascot!

I recommend using this special approach that involves children and their parents in the writing process. Your class mascot will motivate students to write who couldn't have cared less before. The class mascot brings new dimensions to the writing program that will amaze, excite, and regenerate you.

Chapter 12

The Writing Center

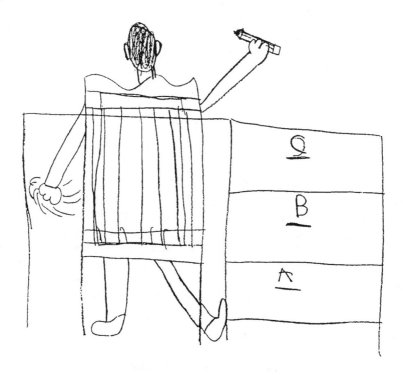

Drawing by Wes Meyer
Third Grade

The writing center is an important addition to a developmentally appropriate, early-writing classroom. The writing center is a place where children go to write during their free time. The writing center in your room inspires highly original and unique kinds of individual writings.

Where To Put a Writing Center

There are several appropriate places for a writing center. Use a long table. Or use a rolling cart with all the writing-center materials so the students can move the center close to their desks for easy access.

A set of shelves also will work. The shelves provide a place to store materials. But they don't allow room to set up typewriters or give kids the space they need when they're feeling very creative.

One teacher who was very short of space came up with a writing-center suitcase. This was a large suitcase filled with writing-center materials. Show the children how to use the materials in the center, then train them carefully how to put the materials away afterwards. The beauty of the writing-center suitcase is that it can be taken out and used, then put away out of sight when children are finished.

Decide that your classroom needs a writing center, and I am confident you will find the place to put it.

Materials

What materials belong in a writing center? Typewriters, (the old manual ones are best), word processing programs (if you use a computer), all kinds of paper, pencils, pens, markers, paints, crayons, ABC stamps, other stamps, stamp pads, lined and unlined paper, graph paper, construction paper (assorted colors), stapler, scotch tape, masking tape, paper punch, a feather pen (like they use at weddings—kids love to write with this pen!), colored pencils, file cards, stationery, envelopes, note pads, small chalk boards, chalk, scissors, pinking shears, stencils, yarn, picture dictionary, wordless books, stickers, story starters, paper clips, rubber bands, wall-paper sample books, paints, and anything else you can find that will encourage kids to write. Look in your desk drawers. I promise you will find many of the materials you need.

Managing the Center

Put up a sign that says: Writing Center or The Write Spot or whatever, so the kids know it is there and that it is important!

Have the kids sign-up if they choose to use it.

The writing center is a good incentive to motivate students to accomplish specified tasks or reinforce good behavior. One time I worked out a deal with one of my students. After he had achieved a scholastic objective upon which we both agreed, his chosen reward was to spend the morning in the writing center.

Assign kids a week day to work in the center. If they choose not to use the center that day, they may pick someone else to take their place. This seldom happens.

Limit the number of children at the center for maximum efficiency. I found three or four in my center was about right.

To introduce the kids to the writing center the teacher should show the whole class the items available. The teacher can explain how certain things in the center operate, like typewriters and computers. She should stress the fact that everything must be put back where it belongs at the end of the center time. I finally decreed that no one went out to recess until all of the center items were back in their proper places.

What Can Kids Do at the Writing Center?

Allow children freedom to use the center however they want. Let them explore and experiment with the materials and utensils. Some teachers assign tasks:

- Type out ABCs, numbers, color words, words from around the room, etc.

- Staple together several pieces of paper and write a story.

- Use temporary spelling on the typewriter or computer for a journal entry.

- The teacher posts a theme-of-the-month on a bulletin board near the writing center. If children can't think of anything to do, they are given writing ideas pertaining to the month's theme.

The kids constructed posters, made cards, wrote letters, wrote thank-you notes, wrote appreciation notes, bound books, wrote poetry, typed out names and alphabet letters, made file folders, wrote and illustrated stories, etc.

Discipline

There weren't any discipline problems at the center. Generally the activities and materials were engaging enough that I didn't even have to monitor the kids who were working there.

Variety of Materials

Don't put everything in the center at once. Rotate materials in the writing center to keep children's interest. Your writing center will resemble a church smorgasbord supper if you put everything out at once. And you know what happens at these suppers! It takes a long time to get through the serving line because there are too many decisions to be made. Limit your students' choices and they will begin work faster.

What About a Take-Home Writing Center?

This is a great idea. Bring a small suitcase the kids can carry comfortably. Put in as many writing materials as it will hold. Assign one child to take it home per night. (Of course, they could decide they didn't want to take it home. That's okay.) The next day the child who has taken it home can share a writing he had accomplished.

Periodically, the writing center suitcase has to be replenished. One easy way to restock supplies is to glue a list of all the materials to the top of the suitcase.

Chapter 13

Wordless Books

Drawing by Mike Mertes
Second Grade

Wordless books are published stories that contain illustrations but no written text. They lend themselves very easily to story writing. Very little teacher motivation is necessary because these books are characterized by provocative illustrations. The student studies the pictures carefully then writes what is happening.

I would recommend these books in late kindergarten for your more able students. Most first graders will be able to use the temporary spelling necessary to complete one of these books.

A list of wordless books appears at the end of this book.

How to Write a Wordless Book

Students have a choice of three options when they participate in this writing strategy:

Option 1: (I recommend this one for kindergarten and first grade.) Copy the pictures from wordless books and paste them on page-size sheets of tagboard, leaving plenty of room for kids to write. Laminate these pages, bind them together with rings, then let students take turns writing the text of the story with a dry-erase pen using temporary spelling.

When they finish writing, let them read it to the class. A copy of each story can be made if the child wants to save it, then wipe the laminated pages clean for the next person. The stories are always different, no matter how many times the children write them.

Option 2: Students write the text for each illustration on plain white paper. Remind students to leave room above or below their text for the copied illustration from the book, which is pasted in later. After the child reads the new book to the class, the book becomes her property, or it can be placed in the school library for posterity.

Option 3: Similar to option 2, but children draw their own illustrations. Students write the text, make the illustrations, bind the books, then share them with the class.

Timing

It's up to the teacher when to use wordless books. I suggest March or April, when you're searching for engaging activities to keep the class motivated.

I recommend using the books during center time so you can keep an eye on kids' progress. Students may want to work on them for several consecutive days. If they're really engrossed in the writing, leave them alone. I can think of nothing more important for them to be doing.

What About Copying Illustrations?
Isn't That Illegal?

Not according to the United States Copyright Law (1976). Permission to copy pictures falls within the definition of "fair use," which allows reproduction for "non-profit educational purposes."

Benefits of the Wordless Books

Writing a wordless book is fun. The pictures often depict highly amusing situations which will titillate the imagination of your most reluctant writers.

Wordless books serve as tremendous motivation to enable children to infer, predict, and analyze the characters, plots, and settings. These books will pique imagination and force your students to create words and descriptions that tell the story. Wordless-book stories enhance children's decision-making skills because the student decides what the characters say and think. Some teachers use the wordless books to reinforce and evaluate the children's learning because while kids are writing text using temporary spelling, they indicate their level of understanding of letters, sounds, and punctuation.

Probably the most important benefit of the wordless books is they give young authors a place to start. Writing a book from scratch is an awesome, overwhelming project that can intimidate budding writers. Any device that helps students through that first page is worthwhile. Students who find writing difficult in other genres will be successfully motivated to write a wordless book.

Chapter 14

Retellings

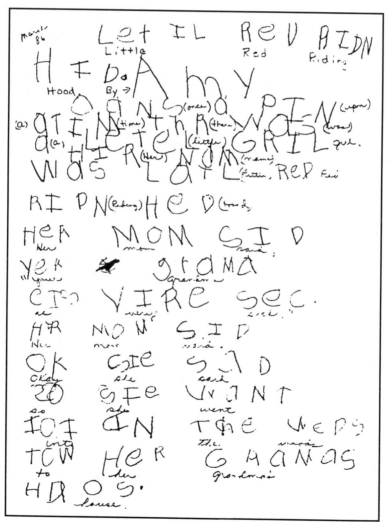

Figure 57: Amy retells the story of <u>Little Red Riding Hood</u>.

Retellings happen when a student simply relates a story he has read or heard, in his own words. Retellings are one of the best ways to check comprehension in older students, and they provide an interesting and engrossing writing activity for your more advanced kindergartners.

Retellings are wonderful for beginning writers because they help the student get started. Decisions about beginnings, story structure, characters, and setting have already been determined by the original story. The child only needs to choose the necessary words to relate the story.

During the first year I used the writing program in kindergarten, I taught a very bright little girl. I had a feeling I was boring her with the usual kindergarten activities. She knew all her letters and sounds and was reading quite well.

One day during center time, I was trying to come up with something that would challenge her. I finally said, "Sharon, why don't you write out your own version of *The Three Bears*"? Her first response was, "I can't spell the words." Even though we had been writing in our journals using temporary spelling for a couple of months, she still felt reluctant to try a whole story. I told her to spell the words the best she knew how, and she ended up writing a several-page version of *The Three Bears*. It kept her meaningfully occupied for many days of center time. After she finished, she shared her story with the whole class, who couldn't help but be impressed with her writing skills.

What happens when kids retell a story? They utilize higher level thinking skills to recall and reconstruct the story. They use visual and auditory memory. Children learn and utilize all literacy skills while writing a retelling. Retelling fires up the kids' imaginations because if they can't remember the exact facts, they make up something that sounds right.

Try a retelling. When you read a student's version of a story, you will be more aware of his abilities to comprehend. Diagnostic information about the child's comprehension taken from retellings is more reliable than contrived questions that follow dull stories in the usual basal comprehension tests. (See Figures 57 and 58).

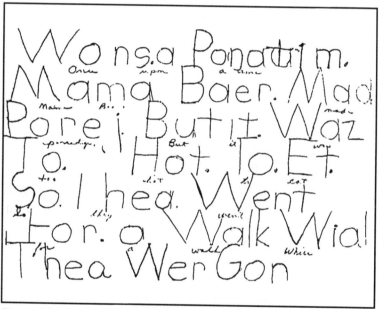

Figure 58: A retelling of _The Three Bears_.

Chapter 15

Extra! Extra!
It's a Kindergarten and
First-Grade Newspaper!

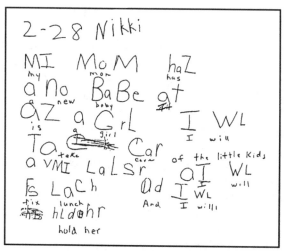

Drawing by Nikki, Kindergarten Student

Drawing by Josh, Kindergarten Student

Most kindergarten and first-grade teachers are not aware that children of this age and developmental level can make class newspapers. I did not make them while I taught kindergarten, but I know several teachers who did.

A simple way to do this is the following: Show the class a newspaper. Point out the logo. Explain to the kids that the logo is kind of like the title of a book. Tell them they're going to make a newspaper too, and that they need a name for it. "Can anyone think of a good name for our class newspaper?" If they can't come up with anything, make several suggestions. Be original. Don't use boring names. *Kindergarten Capers*, or *First Class-First Grade News* are some suggestions to get you going.

After you decide on a name you are ready to begin your news search. I would save the kids' ILESes for several weeks and pick out newsworthy articles from them. A group activity the whole class can do together it to title or headline each one of these articles.

Type these simple articles complete with bylines and datelines. Examine your local papers for any other conventions you need to include to make the class paper appear like a genuine newspaper.

If you don't have time to type the newspaper, have an assistant, parent volunteer, or a secretary help you.

Use a simple two-column format that you find on most word processing programs. I would suggest making the print larger than usual newspaper print because your students will be reading these and the larger print will help.

Have the kids make drawings to go with some of the stories, shrink them so they will fit, and tape them in appropriate places interspersed with the print. You may have to use scissors to do some cutting to get everything in. I tape the original copy of our class   newspaper together, then make a master copy from that.

Your students will be enthusiastic about this project. The whole class enjoys reading the finished product. After the first edition comes out, they will want to do it again.

After the class reads the paper, it is sent home. Copies can be made for other kindergarten and first-grade sections to encourage and acquaint them with the class newspaper.

To keep yourself out of the bind of publishing a newspaper on a certain date, write these words on the front cover next to the logo: *Published Whenever We Get Around To It*. Then if you get another newspaper made, fine, and if you don't, fine!

Give the class newspaper a try. It is a real reason for writing, and your students and their parents will love it.

Go... Write!

Writing's benefits are understood. The rules are known. The resources are available. Writing can be taught daily. There is no excuse for neglecting the teaching of creative writing.

Drawing by Jessica Krahling
Third Grade

Chapter 16

Communicating the Writing Program to Parents

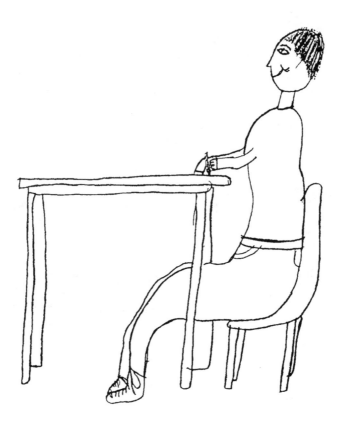

Drawing by Nikki Keller
Third Grade

Communication with parents is crucial to the success of your writing program. When parents know what you're doing and why, they provide important backup and assistance when necessary.

Begin talking to parents about the writing program as early as possible. This puts parents in the picture right away and provides a basis for later communication concerning the writing program. Parents need to know especially about temporary spelling so they don't discourage the child with criticism. An easy way to explain this to parents is to state the following:

"I will be teaching your children to compose stories by writing down the sounds they hear. The words do not have to be spelled correctly because at the beginning I won't be concentrating on spelling, I will be concentrating on PHONICS. While the children are composing their writings, they are learning phonics. Don't be concerned that they might continue to spell the words phonetically. As they come into contact with more printed words, they will notice the difference and change their spelling to match."

A handout easily could be prepared for parents to take home after the first Parents' Night with a brief description of the goals and advantages of the writing program. The Teacher's Digest version of the *Stages of Writing Development* from Chapter 3 also could be included in this handout.

At the beginning of the school year I send home the following letter (see page 131) reminding parents about the writing program: (Feel free to change it to suit your needs.)

How do parents know what's going on in the writing program during the school year? Since I send home very few of the writings during the year (these are stored in colorful student-designed, laminated folders) I keep the parents up-to-date by talking with them face-to-face when they informally drop by the room or during conference time.

At the fall conference in kindergarten, I acquaint them with the journal-writing procedure and ask them to send a spiral notebook (if your school doesn't provide one) with the child by a specific date. As a reminder, I also send out the following note (see page 132):

Dear Parents,

Welcome to the world of kindergarten (or first grade.) Your child will learn so many new things this year I feel I must prepare you for one important area.

I am using a writing program this year that will not only show children how to write but will also help them be better readers later. Research has shown that children taught this way not only learn their readiness and prereading skills more readily but also retain them better.

In the past it was believed that children couldn't learn to read or write until they were taught all their letters and sounds. _Children can write before learning these skills_! They write by dictation, scribbles, drawings, and temporary spelling. When children use the temporary spelling, they write words using the phonetic sounds, usually the consonants first with the vowels added later. In the past we were unaware of the importance of the scribble, drawing, and temporary spelling, but we now know each of these is a normal stage of writing development.

When your children are in school I will encourage them to write using whatever method they think suits them best. Would you please encourage them to write at home also? If your child comes to you with a scribble, drawing, or temporary spelling, ask, "What have you written?" Take the time to print their words before their eyes. Your children will learn so much by your example and by their observation of you accomplishing writing. Don't be concerned (at least for now) with neatness, correct spelling, and punctuation. We'll work on that after the kids are off to a good start. _Do be concerned_ about what the children have communicated to you by their writing. This is the important part.

Please give your children lots of praise, and encourage them to write to relatives and friends. Let them compose the grocery lists and write notes to you. While children write, they read, and use high-level thinking skills. This sets the stage for a productive educational experience.

If you have any questions, I would be delighted to visit with you whenever it is convenient.

Sincerely,
Mrs. Johnson

Dear Parents,

Could you please send a spiral notebook with your child by the end of this week? We will be using these notebooks for journal-writing experiences. The notebook does not need to have wide lines. Regular notebook paper is fine, in fact, preferred.

Thank you for your help,
Mrs. Johnson

At the fall conference, I also urge parents to encourage their children to write at home. Parents can be creative about involving their child in the at-home writing experience. Parents immediately responding to children's notes is one of the best reinforcement procedures I know. Letting a child write the shopping list, which the parent dictates while working around the house, will make the child feel great about writing and will help the parent too. Writing letters to favorite relatives or invitations to parties is always fun for young children.

At the end of the semester, I describe the children's writing development on their report cards. The parents also are kept up-to-date on the children's progress in the take-home journal that Snowball Whiskers uses.

At the end of the year, everything goes home. The Draw-and-Write stories are stapled together in one big book, and the journal goes home as is. This gives the children a special remembrance of their school year. Parents can see and read all the writings composed by the students all by themselves.

For me as a teacher, it is always exciting to read these writings at the end of the year to see the tremendous growth that has taken place. The children themselves seem impressed. As they review all the writings they have accomplished in one year, they realize how far they have come, and their writing confidence blooms.

Chapter 17

Conclusions, Questions, and Answers

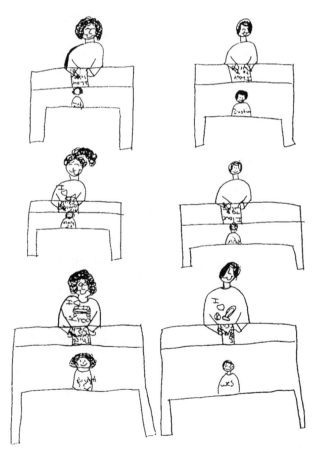

Drawing by Bridget Prins
Third Grade

I wonder now how I taught kindergarten for ten years without using the writing program in my classroom.

Writing should be taught as a legitimate part of the early childhood curriculum. The writing experience is valuable to kindergarten and first grade children because it introduces them to print as a natural part of their learning environment. Children taught to write in kindergarten and first grade learn visual discrimination skills more readily because writing encourages cognitive processes which produce higher learning levels. Students know their sounds and letters better when the teacher uses the writing program. More importantly, they develop an understanding of why they need to know letters and sounds. This knowledge will translate into end-of-year test results that will surprise you.

What's This Going to Cost Me?

A teacher who seeks to sell this program to a principal, curriculum committee, school board, or a parent advisory board should have no trouble because of the low cost factor.

The following items are the only instructional materials necessary to teach my writing program:

1) this book

2) large tablets

3) colored felt-tipped markers

4) 12" x 18" story paper

5) school-constructed, plain white paper writing journals (or have the kids bring their own)

When Should I Have the Children Write?

As you try each writing strategy, note how long the procedure takes. (Each class responds differently, so I can't give you a hard-and-fast rule on this.) When you know how much time each one takes your class, look at your schedule and place each strategy where it best fits.

Some research leads us to believe the most successful writing occurs earlier in the day. The children are fresher, exhibit clearer thinking, have more innovative ideas, and express their feelings more adequately in the morning.

But if it's later-or-never, write whenever you can find the time.

What Should be the Timetable for Introducing the Different Writing Strategies?

In kindergarten start the ILES the first day, and do one every day.

Add the Draw and Write whenever you finish a unit, about once a month.

Start journal writing in late October, at least three times a week. If you have an all-day-every-day program, journal each day.

Pick and choose from the rest of the strategies whenever you need to revive class interest with something new and exciting. Some years you may use all of the strategies, while other years, just a few. It depends a lot on your class. You don't need to use all the strategies to have a successful writing program. The important thing to remember is to write every day.

In first grade follow the same procedure that kindergarten uses, but start journaling right away.

What if the Program Isn't Carried on in Later Grades?

This question is often raised by teachers. Writing experts say that because writing does enhance readiness, pre-reading, thinking, communication, decision-making, etc., the teaching of writing can only benefit children in later years. In any event, the writing experience can't hurt.

How Do I Find Time to Write?

Some teachers feel they have no time to write. I say they don't have time *not* to write. Writing cannot be left out or given leftover time. Because of writing's intimate involvement with all areas of the curriculum, it must be done!

To help use your time in a more efficient manner, carefully peruse your curriculum. Throw out all activities that are nice but don't really enhance the child's total education experience as writing does.

Remember, don't teach writing as a separate skill. Use it in all areas of the curriculum. Be creative and find new ways to utilize writing even during math time. (Have children write beginning story problems using the math skills you are teaching.)

Many schools in our area have mandatory silent reading time for the first 20 minutes of each day. Because children are reading when they are writing, there is no reason they cannot be writing for part of this reading time.

One second-grade teacher told me that the minute her children come into the classroom they take out their journals and start writing.

After they finish, they take out their library books and read quietly for the rest of the time period.

Use the writing program with your readiness series. Probably the only change you need to make is to use the writing activities for skill reinforcement instead of the numerous worksheets and workbook pages teachers usually assign.

How Much Correcting Should I Do on the Kids' Writing? If I Follow Your Rules and Note Only the Content, Won't Parents Think I'm Not Doing a Good Job?

A teacher who tries to correct all the children's writing used in my program will not have enough time.

Do not feel you have to correct their writing. Celebrate kids' writing, rather than correct it.

Remember, in kindergarten and first grade, the philosophy is to let children write. If you red-mark them, you will inhibit the vital freshness of their writing. Study Chapter 4's rules.

Don't feel you have to send any of the writing home. The ILES is the exception to this. Save all the rest until the end of the year. Share them with parents at conferences and during report card time, noting how the child is progressing. Otherwise all writing stays in school. Encourage parents to come to school and see the children's writing at any time.

What Do You Do About Children Who Write the Same Message Every Day?

This is a problem that did not happen to me until the third year I used the writing program. That year I was confronted by one child who wrote the following entry every day: "I went to see my grandma." During conferencing I tried to elicit a different response by asking every question under the sun about why the visit to grandma's was so important, but for a long time nothing changed. Then towards the end of the year, new subjects started appearing in the journal. When that happened, I strongly commended the child for the new information.

I urge teachers to be patient in cases like this. Wait for the child to take one step in a positive direction. When that occurs, immediately reinforce the move with numerous affirming words and actions.

It takes some children longer than others to feel secure with you. Until that time they will continue to write something "safe." The best thing a teacher can do in this situation is be patient and reassuring.

What Do You Do with Children Who Produce the Same Type of Writing All the Time?

This is a real toughie. Again, this problem did not happen to me until the third year I used the writing program. Two of my students began writing horror stories filled with "blood and killings." This went on and on. At first I accepted all of their entries though they did not seem quite appropriate for kindergarten children.

I finally checked with the school psychologist. He told me this "blood and killing" theme was fairly common in many children's stories, books, videos, and TV programs. He said it was not unusual for kids to pick up on the violence. I asked if this indicated something dangerous. He replied that if children were simply writing about violence and not acting it out, it probably was just a phase. He did tell me to talk to the children's parents and tell them what I had observed. He also said to suggest that the children not be allowed to view the "horror-type" of movies or TV programs.

I followed his suggestions and the parents were most cooperative. At the same time, whenever these particular children made any move to write any other type of journal entry, I strongly commended their choice.

Eventually the horror stories did end, and both children happily moved on to explore the many other areas of subject matter.

Do You Give Any Instruction on Sentence Construction?

Of course, good teachers model sentence structure all the time as they read and write in front of the children. Towards the end of the kindergarten year, start talking about "What is a sentence?"

For example, a simplified definition would be a group of words that tell about someone or something and what that someone or something is doing. Have children evaluate sentences and sentence fragments. Discuss the fact that sentences begin with a capital letter and end with a period, question mark, or exclamation point.

Draw the children's attention to the number of sentences in their ILESes by counting them in front of the class. Ask, "How many sentences are there in this story?" After a while, some catch on, but others are not ready for this yet.

Better to teach the concept of a sentence at the first-grade level. Kindergarten students can use sentence structure correctly but they have no idea why they are doing it.

The most difficult part of the first-grade teacher's job is to teach the children how to form a complete sentence and punctuate and capitalize it correctly. It seems strange to do this after the kids have written for a year in kindergarten. But it is a skill that needs to be learned, and it does give the children a better idea of why they're doing what they are doing.

Note the sentences children write. They never use the simplistic sentence structure commonly used in a vast amount of the early-basal-reading series. Peruse the children's writings contained in this book. You will not find one, "See Dick. See Dick run!" type communication. The children consistently use long flowing sentences to communicate their thoughts in a natural way.

What can basal-reading-book authors learn by observing the way kids write? I think we insult children's intelligence by giving them short, stilted, unnatural sentences in their first readers. It would not be impossible for the child to develop mixed-up conceptions about sentence construction from the example of the sentences in these early "stories."

What Do You Think About Teaching Editing and Revision Skills In Kindergarten and First Grade?

This question comes up regularly at writing workshops I conduct. Generally, my philosophy for kindergarten and first grade is *Let them write!*

The fewer things we do to halt the free flow of ideas at this developmental level, the better. Editing and rewriting skills are usually touched on in the second grade, but third grade is the place to teach all the steps of revision. The third-grade developmental level is ready and able to handle this procedure.

Kindergarten and first-grade children need not concern themselves with correcting errors in spelling, punctuation, capitalization, etc. Follow the writing-workshop guidelines in this book, and just enjoy, encourage, and appreciate the children's writing efforts.

To every rule there is an exception. What do you do with a gifted child who is ready at an earlier time for the editing experience? What about an overzealous, perfectionistic child who insists on getting it all right? Sometimes schools require first graders to submit writing to young authors contests. What do you do then? Let your expertise and common sense guide you.

How Does a Teacher Manage to Write all that is Dictated When the Child Speaks with "Machine Gun" Bursts of Words?

An additional dimension to this problem is the need to provide a good model of proper letter formation and a neat finished product while printing as fast as you can.

This is a problem that occurs frequently. Quietly tell the child to slow down because you can't write as fast as they're talking. They must become aware of the fact that our speech and thoughts are produced more rapidly than we can write them on paper. Learning patience is a positive experience.

Another idea is to take down the fast talker's words in shorthand (of a sort). Just write the child's message on notes that adhere to the journal page. Later the teacher can transcribe the child's dictation into the journal, preferably in the child's presence.

What if I Don't Have Time for Conferences With Every Child, Every Day?

During a writing workshop one teacher mentioned this problem. She said she had solved it by assigning children certain days of the week for a conference. She said her students wrote every day, but only met with her on their assigned day.

Teachers have large classes and a tight schedule. I can understand why this teacher felt she had to do this. But I also feel something else could have been deleted from her schedule rather than this very important step in journal writing.

In the ideal situation teachers meet with each child every day for the following reasons:

- Young children do forget what they have written overnight and even after a few hours. A child may write a very important message to the teacher in the journal, but the teacher would miss it because it was not that particular child's day to have a conference. When I think of some of the messages my students communicate to me, I would hate to take that chance.

- If the child has a conference only once a week, the positive aspects of writing that enhance a child's self-esteem are weakened.

But, if your class size, length of day, or curriculum requirements severely limit your time, and you feel like you must conference once a week or not at all, do what you have to do! The children still benefit from the conferences you are able to hold.

What Effect Does Writing Have on a Child's Vocabulary?

I kept track of the vocabulary words used in two of my students' writing projects for a three-month period for two consecutive years. Each year I would select a super-sharp student and a struggler to observe.

The first year the sharp student used 227 words, and the struggler used 156 words during the three-month period.

The next year, I again chose a sharp student and a struggler from my kindergarten class. During year two, the sharp student used 222 words and the struggler used 248.

It needs to be understood that both of the sharp students were writing their words using temporary spelling, and the two strugglers dictated all their words after scribbling or drawing in their journals.

I had expected there would be a larger difference between the strugglers and the sharp students. I was wrong. When kids are allowed to work at their own developmental level, they accomplish important educational goals.

I was surprised at how many words they were using. Usually at the end of kindergarten, we expect children to know and be able to use 20 words at the most. The thought occurred to me, that we probably insult the intelligence of children when we expect them to know 20 words when they routinely use more than 200.

The writing program gives everyone a chance. Even though some students start off the year advanced in many ways, the children coming into school who have minimal exposure to school skills are still able to have a successful experience with writing.

Have You Experienced Any Serious Problems with This Writing Program?

Only one problem occurred that you may need to worry about. Two months before school ended several of my students said they didn't want to be promoted to first grade. "Why?" I asked. "We want to stay with you," they all said in unison.

A unique closeness develops between teacher and student when you use my writing program. It makes it tough to let them go at the end of the year. Luckily, I was able to convince them that promotion was for the best, but I did recognize their feelings because I felt the same way. I don't think I'll ever find an answer to this particular problem.

Is It Okay to Write on Kids' Writing? Doesn't This Take Away Their Ownership?

I have spoken personally about this subject to Donald Graves, Lucy Calkins, Anne Haas Dyson, and Jan Turbill. *They say it is okay to write on your students' writing.*

I write on journal entries when words aren't clear because otherwise, the child's content would be lost.

I never use a red pencil when I write my notes. Most of the time they pay no attention to my printing. If they do ask what I'm doing, I tell them, "These marks will help me remember your clever words!" They never get the idea I'm correcting them. I'm not. I'm saving content.

But having said all that, if a child would say, "Don't write on my writing!" I wouldn't. Perhaps a sticky note could be used at that time to save content.

Have You Got Any Final Thoughts About the Writing Program?

I encourage you to start a writing program. From the contents of this book you can see how much joy the teaching of writing has brought into my life. It is genuine fun! I dread to think what I would have missed if I had never tried it.

I received the following letter from a teacher who attended one of my workshops. I have her permission to share it with you because it fits right in with what I've been talking about:

Dear Mrs. Johnson,

I had written to you last fall and thanked you for the wonderful ideas you shared at your workshop in Cedar Rapids.

Once again I want to thank you for being such an inspiration for me. This past year has been the most productive and satisfying year I have ever had. (I've been teaching ten years). I have looked forward to each day! We've kept journals and written numerous books. The kids are so excited about writing, we even started a writers club, which meets Wednesdays after school.

Up 'til this year, I was beginning to feel burned out. I knew something was missing. Your workshop provided me with the missing link...writing!

This next school year will provide even more challenges and rewards. I have accepted a teaching position at Malcolm Price Lab. School at the University of Northern Iowa in Cedar Falls. I will be teaching first grade. I can't wait.

I truly believe if I had not attended your workshop and been given the stepping stones to begin writing, I would not have had the year that I had, nor have the courage to face the exciting challenges at the Lab School.

Thank you so much!

Sincerely,
Mary Kathleen Schneider

Don't be afraid to start a writing program like Mary Kathleen did. If she can do it and I can do it, you can do it. Don't give up once you start. Hang in there. The rewards are worth the trouble.

What About Other Teachers? Won't I Get a Bad Time About Teaching Writing This Way?

The answer to that is a question: Are you teaching school to impress other teachers, or are you there to lead students into the greatest literacy experience of their lives?

Take a risk. Do what you know to be right. You can't go wrong with that advice.

Happy writing!!

Wordless Books List

Alexander, Martha. *Out! Out! Out!* Dial Books, N.Y.

Anno, Mitsumasa. *Anno's Britain* Philomel Books

Anno's Counting Book Crowell

Anno's Counting House Philomel Books

Anno's USA Philomel Books

Aruego, Jose. *We Hide, You Seek* Greenwillow Books

Barner, Bob. *The Elephant's Visit* Little

Briggs, Raymond. *The Snowman* Random House

Carle, Eric. *One, Two, Three to the Zoo* World Pub.

The Secret Birthday Message Crowell

Carroll, Ruth. *What Whiskers Did* Walck

Carroll, Ruth and Latrobe. *The Christmas Kitten* Walck

Crews, Donald. *Truck* Greenwillow Books

De Paola, Tomie. *The Hunter and the Animals* Holiday House

Pancakes for Breakfast Harcourt, Brace, Jovanovich

Florian, Douglas. *The City* Crowell

Goodall, John S. *The Adventures of Paddy Pork* Atheneum

Paddy Goes Traveling Atheneum

Paddy Pork, Odd Jobs Atheneum

Hoban, Tana. *Is it Rough? Is it Smooth? Is it Shiny?*

Look Again! Greenwillow Books

Hogrogrian, Nonny. *Apples* Harper Collins

Keats, Ezra Jack. *Clementina's Cactus* Viking Press

Krahn, Fernando. *April Fools* Dutton

Arthur's Adventures in an Abandoned House Dutton

Mayer, Mercer. *Ah-Choo* Dial Press

Hiccup Dial Press

Omerod, Jan. *Moonlight* Lothrop, Lee & Shepard

Spier, Peter. *Christmas* Doubleday, NY

Rain Doubleday, NY

Stoddard, Darrell. *The Hero* Argo

Ungerer, Tomi. *Snail, Where Are You?* Harper

Ward, Lynd. *The Silver Pony* Houghton Mifflin

Winter, Paula. *The Bear and the Fly* Crown Publishing

(This is by no means a complete listing of all the wordless books available. These particular titles were the ones I found in our school library. Your librarian will assist you in locating others).

Periodicals That Publish Children's Writing

Chickadee. The Young Naturalist Foundation. 59 Front Street, E. Toronto, Ontario MSE 1B3 Canada. (Age range 4-8. The environment. Accepts letters for "Something to Chirp About," a monthly feature.)

Children's Digest. P.O. Box 576B, Indianapolis, IN 46206. (Age range 8-10. Health, Safety, and Nutrition. Accepts poetry, jokes, riddles, stories up to 700 words. In "What Do You Think?" children write about questions asked in earlier issues.)

Child Life. P.O. Box 576B, Indianapolis, IN 46206. (Age range 7-9. Health, Safety, and Nutrition. Accepts poetry, stories up to 500 words, jokes and riddles. "All Yours" features letters to the editor.)

Children's Playmate. P.O. Box 576B, Indianapolis, IN 46206. (Age range 5-7. Accepts artwork and poetry.)

Cricket. P.O. Box 100, La Salle, IL 61301. (Age range 6-12. Literary. Accepts children's contributions for "Letterbox" and "Cricket League." Cricket League contests are held monthly in two or three categories—drawing, poetry, and short story. Rules for the contests are explained in each issue.)

Ebony Jr! 820 S. Michigan Ave., Chicago, IL 60605. (Children. Accepts original poems, short stories, essays, jokes, riddles, cartoons, and artwork.)

The Electric Company. 200 Watt Street, P.O. Box 2924, Boulder CO 80322. (Age range 6-9. General interest. Unsolicited material accepted, including jokes for "Tickle Yourself." Specific guidelines for other contributions such as poetry, short stories and essays appear in each issue.)

Humpty Dumpty. P.O. Box 567B, Indianapolis, IN 46206. (Age range 4-6. Health, Safety, and Nutrition. Accepts children's artwork.)

Highlights for Children. 803 Church St., Honsdale, PA 18431. (Age range 2-12. General interest. Accepts original poetry, short stories, jokes, riddles, brief personal narratives, letters to the editor and "Creatures Nobody Has Ever Seen." All contributions are acknowledged with an extremely kind letter.)

Jack and Jill. P.O. Box 567B, Indianapolis, IN 46206. (Age range 6-8. Health, Safety, and Nutrition. Accepts artwork, poetry, jokes and riddles, letters to the editor, and short stories up to 500 words.)

Turtle. P.O. Box 567B, Indianapolis, IN 46206. (Age range 2-5. Accepts children's art work.)

Pennywhistle Press. Box 500-P, Washington, D.C. 20044. (Age range 4-12. General interest. Weekly. Accepts drawings, jokes, riddles, and letters to "Mailbag." Contests are also held periodically.)

The McGuffey Writer. 400 A McGuffey Hall. Miami University, Oxford, OH 45056. (Age range preschool through 18. Children's writing. Accepts poetry, cartoons and art as well as short stories and essays. Word limit is two typewritten pages. Longer works are often excerpted.)

Stone Soup. Children's Art Foundation, P.O. Box 83, Santa Cruz, CA 95063. (Age range 6-13. Literary. Accepts poetry, short stories, drawings, and book reviews. Longer works that describe personal experiences are encouraged. Children interested in doing book reviews should address their correspondence to Jerry Mandel. Stone Soup will provide the book to be reviewed.)

Wombat. Journal of Young People's Writing and Art. 365 Ashton Drive, Athens, GA 30606. (Age range 6-18. Young people's creative work in art and writing. Accepts original poetry, short stories, prose, essays, artwork (black and white preferred or color with strong line definition), cartoons, puzzles and book reviews.)

Pattern Books List

Aardema, V. *Why Mosquitoes Buzz in People's Ears.* Dial Books For Young Readers.

Allard, H. *I Will Not Go To Market Today.* Dial Books For Young Readers.

Allen, Pamela. *Bertie and the Bear.* Putnam Publishing.

Allison, Beverly. *Mitzi's Magic Garden.* Thomas Nelson Publishing.

Barret, Judi. *A Snake is Totally Tall.* Atheneum Publishing, New York.

Barret, Judi. *What's Left?* Atheneum Publishing, New York.

Barton, Byron. *Buzz, Buzz, Buzz.* Penguin.

Bauer, C. F. *My Mom Travels a Lot.* Frederick Warne and Company, New York.

Bayer, Jane. *My Name is Alice.* Dial Books For Young Readers.

Baylor, Byrd. *Everybody Needs a Rock.* Scribner, New York.

Blair, S. *The Three Billy Goats Gruff.* Holt, Rinehart and Winston, New York.

Borton, Helen. *Do You Know What I Know?* Abellard-Schuman, New York.

Bowers, K. R. *At This Very Moment.* Little and Brown, Berkely, California.

Boynton, Sandra. *If At First.* Little Brown and Company, New York.

Bradfield, Roger. *Hello Rock.* Wester Publishing Company.

Brooke, L. Leslie. *Johnny Crow's Garden*. Frederick Warne and Company, New York.

Brooke, L. Leslie. *Johnny Crow's New Garden*. Frederick Warne and Company, NY.

Brown, Margaret Wise. *The Important Book*. Harper and Row, New York.

Brown, Margaret Wise. *The Runaway Bunny*. Harper and Row, New York.

Burningham, John. *Would You Rather?* Harper and Row, New York.

Byars, Betsy. *Go and Hush the Baby*. Viking Press, California.

Cameron, Polly. *I Can't Said the Ant*. Scholastic Book Service, New York.

Campbell, Rod. *Dear Zoo*. Four Winds Press, New York.

Carle, Eric. *The Grouchy Lady Bug*. Thomas Y. Crowell Publishing.

Charlip, Remy. *Fortunately*. Four Winds Press, New York.

Charlip, Remy. *Mother, Mother I Feel Sick*. Scholastic Books, New York.

Chess, Victoria. *Poor Esme*. Holiday House.

Cook, Lyn. *If I Were All These*. Burns and MacEacheran.

De Regniers, B. *May I Bring a Friend?* Atheneum, New York.

De Regniers, B. *What Can You Do With a Shoe?* Harper and Row, New York.

Digby, Desmond. *Waltzing Matilda*. Collins, London.

Domanska, Janine. *Busy Monday Morning*. Green Willow Books.

Domanska, Janine. *If All the Seas Were One Sea*. Macmillan Publishing, New York.

Einsel, Walter. *Did You Ever See?* Scholastic Book Service, New York.

Ellentuck, Shan. *The Upside Down Man*. Doubleday, New York.

Elting, M. and Folsum, M. *Q is For Duck*. Houton Mifflin Company, Massachusetts.

Emberly, Barbara. *One Wild River to Cross*. Scholastic Books, New York.

Emberly, Ed. *Klippety Klop*. Little Brown Publishing, New York.

Ets, Marie Hall. *Elephant in a Well*. Viking Children's Books.

Gag, Wanda. *Millions of Cats*. Putnam Publishing.

Hanlon, Emily. *What If a Lion Eats Me or ...?* Delacorte Press, New York.

Hoban, Russel. *Nothing to Do*. Scholastic Books, New York.

Hoberman, M. A. *A House is a House For Me*. Viking Penguin, New York.

Hogrogrian, Nonny. *One Fine Day*. Collier.

Horwitz, Elinor. *When The Sky Is Lace*. Harper and Row, New York.

Houguet, S. R. *I Unpacked My Grandmother's Trunk*. E. P. Dutton.

Hutchins, Pat. *Don't Forget the Bacon*. Penguin.

Hutchins, Pat. *Good Night Owl*. Macmillan, New York.

Jacobs, Leland. *Good Night Mr. Beetle*. Holt, Rinehart, and Winston, New York.

Jeffers, Susan. *All the Pretty Horses*. Macmillan, New York.

Katz, Bobbi. *Nothing But a Dog*. The Feminist Press.

Keats, E. J. *Over in the Meadow*. Four Winds Press, New York.

Kent, Jack. *The Fat Cat*. Scholastic Books, New York.

Kellogg, Steven. *Can I Keep Him?* Dial Press, New York.

Krauss, Ruth. *Everything Under a Mushroom*. Scholastic Book Service, New York.

Krauss, Ruth. *Is This You?* Scholastic Book Service, New York.

Krauss, Ruth. *Mama I Wish I Was Snow-Children You'd Be Cold*. Atheneum, NY.

Kuskin, Karla. *The Philharmonic Gets Dressed*. Harper and Row, New York.

Kuskin, Karla. *Just Like Everyone Else*. Harper and Row, New York.

Leman, Martin. *Comic and Curious Cats*. Crown Publishing, New York.

Lionni, Leo. *A Color of His Own*. Pantheon Books, Toronto.

Lobel, A. *The Ice Cream Coot and Other Rare Birds*. Four Winds Press, New York.

Lobel, Arnold. *The Rose in my Garden*. Greenwillow Books.

Lobel, N and Farber, N. *As I Was Crossing Boston Common*. Creative Arts Books.

Martin Jr., Bill. *America I Know You*. Bowmar Press, California.

Martin Jr., Bill. *Brown Bear, Brown Bear*. Holt, Rinehart and Winston, New York.

Martin Jr., Bill. *David Was Mad*. Holt, Rinehart and Winston, New York.

Martin Jr., Bill. *I Am Freedom's Child*. Bowmar Press, California.

Martin Jr., Bill. *My Days Are Made of Butterflies*. Holt, Rinehart, and Winston, NY.

Martin Jr., Bill. *Poor Old Uncle Sam*. Bowmar Press, California.

Martin Jr., Bill. *The Turning of the Year*. Holt, Rinehart and Winston, New York.

Martin Jr., Bill. *Whistle Mary, Whistle*. Holt, Rinehart and Winston, New York.

Mizumura, K. *If I Were a Cricket*. Thomas Y. Crowell Publishing.

Most, B. *If the Dinosaurs Came Back*. Harcourt, Brace and Jovanovitch, California.

Mumeroff, L. J. *If You Give a Mouse a Cookie*. Harper and Row, New York.

Noble, Trinka Hakes. *The Day Jimmy's Boa Ate the Wash*. Dial Books for Young Readers.

Noble, Trinka Hakes. *Jimmy's Boa Bounces Back*. Dial Books For Young Readers.

O'Neill, Mary. *Hailstones and Halibut Bones*. Doubleday and Company, New York.

Parish, Peggy. *Amelia Bedelia*. Scholastic Book Service, New York.

Parker, Nancy. *Love From Aunt Betty*. Dodd, Mead and Company, New York.

Pearson, T. C. *Old MacDonald Had a Farm*. Dial Books For Young Readers.

Preston, Edna. *The Temper Tantrum Book*. Viking, New York.

Seuss, Dr. *And To Think That I Saw It on Mulberry Street*. Vanguard Press, New York.

Seuss, Dr. *Green Eggs and Ham*. Beginner Books.

Shaw, Charles. *It Looked Like Spilled Milk*. Macmillan Publishing, New York.

Silverstein, Shel. *A Giraffe and a Half*. Harper and Row, New York.

Silverstein, Shel. *Who Wants a Cheap Rhinoceros?* Macmillan Publishing, New York.

Sullivan, J. *Round is a Pancake*. Holt, Rinehart and Winston, New York.

Stevens, Janet. *The House That Jack Built*. Holiday House.

Tanz, Christine. *An Egg is to Sit On*. Lothrup, Lee and Shepard Books.

Tolstoy, Alexi. *The Great, Big, Enormous Turnip*. Franklin Watts.

Udry, Janice. *A Tree is Nice*. Harper and Row, New York.

Uppenheim, Joanne. *Have You Seen Trees?* Young Scott Books, New York.

Van Allsburg, Chris. *The Mysteries of Harris Burdick*. Houton Mifflin Company.

Vigna, J. *Couldn't We Have a Turtle Instead?* Whitman and Company, New York.

Viorst, Judith. *Alexander and the Terrible, Horrible, No-Good, Very Bad Day*. Atheneum, New York.

Viorst, Judith. *I'll Fix Anthony*. Harper and Row, New York.

Viorst, Judith. *My Mama Says There Aren't Any Zombies...Etc*. Atheneum, New York.

Westcott, N. B. *I Know An Old Lady Who Swallowed a Fly*. Little Brown Publishing.

Williams, Barbara. *If He's My Brother*. Prentice-Hall Inc., New Jersey.

Wilson, R. *Ziggy's Lucky Unlucky Book*. American Greeting Cards.

Worstell, V. *Jump the Rope Jingles*. Collier, New York.

Wright, H. R. *A Maker of Boxes*. Holt, Rinehart and Winston, New York.

Wyler, Rose. *The Riddle Kingdom*. Scholastic Books, New York.

Zolotow, Charlotte. *But Not Billy*. Harper and Row, New York.

Zolotow, Charlotte. *Janey*. Harper and Row, New York.

Zolotow, Charlotte. *Do You Know What I'll Do?* Harper and Row, New York.

Zolotow, Charlotte. *If It Weren't For You*. Harper and Row, New York.

Zolotow, Charlotte. *May I Visit?* Harper and Row, New York.

Zolotow, Charlotte. *My Friend John*. Harper and Row, New York.

Zolotow, Charlotte. *Some Day*. Harper and Row, New York.

Zolotow, Charlotte. *Some Things Go Together*. Harper and Row, New York.

References

Atkins, C. (1984, November). Writing: Doing something constructive. Young Children, 40(1), pp. 3-5.

Calkins, L.M. (1983, September). Making the reading and writing connection. Learning, 12(2), pp. 82-86.

Durkins, D. (1971). Children who read early. New York: Teacher's College Press.

Durkin, D. (1971). Teaching them to read. Boston: Allyn and Bacon, Inc.

Dyson, A.H. (1981, October). Oral language: The rooting system for learning to write. Language Arts, 58(7), pp. 776-784.

Dyson, S.H. (1985, March). Three emergent writers and the school curriculum. Elementary School Journal, 85(4), 497-512.

Emig, J. (1977, May). Writing as a mode of learning. College Composition and Communication, 28(2), pp. 122-128.

Gibbs, V.M. (1983). Reading: The core of learning. Proceedings of the Annual Reading Conference (13th), Indiana State University, Terre Haute Curriculum Research and Development Center.

Graves, D. (1978). Balance the basics: Let them write. A Report to the Ford Foundation, pp. 10-11.

Hall, M.A. (1981). Teaching reading as a language experience. Columbus, Ohio: Charles E. Merrill Publishing Company.

Hall, M.A. (1978). The language experience approach to teaching reading. Urbana, Illinois: ERIC Clearinghouse on Reading and communication Skills.

Hazlewood School District. (1969). Language arts guide, kindergarten through level twelve. Hazlewood, Missouri: Author.

Hipple, M.L. (1985, March). Journal writing in the kindergarten. Language Arts, 62(3), pp. 255-261.

Kamii, C. (1985, September). Leading primary education to excellence: Beyond worksheets and drill. Young Children, 40(6), pp. 3-9.

Koeller, S. (1984, May/June). Challenging language experience: The project approach versus "Reeling and Writhing". Childhood Education, 60(5), pp. 331-335.

List, H. (1984, January). Kids can write the day they start school. Early Years, 14(5), pp. 31-33

Morris, J.K. (1984, April/May). Raising their voices: A way to make writing matter to kids. Learning, 12(9), pp. 37-38.

Ollila, L., & Mayfield, M., & Williams, B. (1982, September). A study of the creative writing of grade one level children in England, the United States and Canada. NCTE Newsletter: The International Assembly, 15-23.

Piazza, C.L. & Tomlinson, C.M. (1985, February). A concert of writers. Language Arts, 62(2), pp. 150-158.

Sowers, S. (1980, October). Kds on rit. Learning, 9(3), pp. 14, 18.

Smith, F. (1981, October). Myths of writing. Language Arts, 58(7), pp. 792-797.

Starvish, M. (1984, April/May). A delicate art of helping very young writers. Learning, 12(9), pp. 40-41.

Wallace, J.M. (1985, February). Write first, then read. Educational Leadership, 42(5), pp. 20-24.

Walshe, R.D. (Ed.). (1982). Children want to write. Heinemann Educational Books.

Wiseman, D.L. (1984, January). Helping children take early steps toward reading and writing. The Reading Teacher, 37(4), pp. 340-344.